Perhaps no other Christians are so identified with the importance of prayer in the life of the believer than George Müller and R.A. Torrey.

Now for the first time, two classics on the subject: ANSWERS TO PRAYER and HOW TO PRAY, are together in one volume.

In clear, straightforward fashion, Müller and Torrey outline what the Bible teaches about prayer. Find out how much a real understanding of their teachings can greatly enrich your Christian life.

THE CHRISTIAN LIBRARY has been designed and produced for the discerning book lover. These classics of the Christian faith have been printed and bound with beauty, readability and longevity in mind. Greatest care has gone into the selection of these volumes, with the hope that you will not only find books that are a joy to read, but books that will stir your faith and enlighten your daily walk with the Lord.

Books Available include:

ABIDE IN CHRIST, Andrew Murray
ABSOLUTE SURRENDER, Andrew Murray
AT THE BACK OF THE NORTH WIND,
George MacDonald
BEN-HUR: A TALE OF THE CHRIST, Lew Wallace
CHRISTIAN'S SECRET OF A HAPPY LIFE,
Hannah Whitall Smith
CONFESSIONS OF ST. AUGUSTINE
THE CROSS AND THE SWITCHBLADE, David Wilkerson
DAILY LIGHT
EACH NEW DAY, Corrie ten Boom
FOXE'S CHRISTIAN MARTYRS OF THE WORLD,
GOD AT EVENTIDE, A.J. Russell
GOD CALLING, A.J. Russell
GOD'S SMUGGLER, Brother Andrew
GOD OF ALL COMFORT, Hannah Whitall Smith
GRACE ABOUNDING, John Bunyan
GREAT WOMEN OF THE CHRISTIAN FAITH,
Edith Deen
HIDING PLACE, THE, Corrie ten Boom
HINDS' FEET ON HIGH PLACES, Hannah Hurnard
HOW TO PRAY/ANSWERS TO PRAYER, Torrey and Müller
THE IMITATION OF CHRIST, Thomas A. Kempis
IN HIS STEPS, Charles M. Sheldon
JOSEPHUS 39 B.C. TO 70 A.D.
MERE CHRISTIANITY, C.S. Lewis
MY UTMOST FOR HIS HIGHEST, Oswald Chambers
THE PILGRIM'S PROGRESS, John Bunyan
POWER THROUGH PRAYER/
PURPOSE IN PRAYER, E.M. Bounds
QUIET TALKS ON PRAYER, S.D. Gordon
THE REALITY OF THE CROSS OF CHRIST, T.A. Sparks
SCREWTAPE LETTERS, C.S. Lewis
THE TREASURY OF CHRISTIAN CLASSICS
WHO'S WHO IN THE BIBLE, Frank S. Mead
WITH CHRIST IN THE SCHOOL OF PRAYER,
Andrew Murray

HOW TO PRAY

by

R.A. Torrey

ANSWERS TO PRAYER

by

George Müller

TWO BOOKS IN ONE

BARBOUR AND COMPANY, INC.
164 Mill Street
Westwood, New Jersey 07675

©1989 by Barbour and Company, Inc.

All rights reserved. No part of this publication may be reproduced or transmitted in any form or by any means without written permission of the publisher.

ISBN 1-55748-012-5

Published by: **BARBOUR AND COMPANY, INC.**
164 Mill Street
Westwood, New Jersey 07675

(In Canada, THE CHRISTIAN LIBRARY,
960 The Gateway, Burlington, Ontario L7L 5K7)

EVANGELICAL CHRISTIAN PUBLISHERS ASSOCIATION ecpa MEMBER

Printed in the United States of America

HOW TO PRAY

by
R.A. Torrey

CONTENTS

CHAPTER	PAGE
I. The Importance of Prayer	1
II. Praying unto God	13
III. Obeying and Praying	17
IV. Praying in the Name of Christ and According to the Will of God	21
V. Praying in the Spirit	26
VI. Always Praying and Not Fainting	29
VII. Abiding in Christ	32
VIII. Praying with Thanksgiving	35
IX. Hindrances to Prayer	37
X. When to Pray	44
XI. The Need of a General Revival	48
XII. The Place of Prayer Before and During Revivals	55

HOW TO PRAY

Chapter I
THE IMPORTANCE OF PRAYER

In the 6th chapter of Ephesians in the 18th verse we read words which put the tremendous importance of prayer with startling and overwhelming force:

"Praying always with all prayer and supplication in the Spirit, and watching thereunto with all perseveverance and supplication for all saints."

When we stop to weigh the meaning of these words, then note the connection in which they are found, the intelligent child of God is driven to say,

"I must pray, pray, pray. I must put all my energy and all my heart into prayer. Whatever else I do, I must pray."

The Revised Version is, if possible, stronger than the Authorized:

"With all prayer and supplication praying at all seasons in the Spirit, and watching thereunto in all perseverance and supplication for all the saints."

Note the *alls*: "with *all* prayer," "at *all* seasons," "in *all* perseverance," "for *all* the saints." Note the piling up of strong words, "prayer," "supplication," "perseverance." Note once more the strong expression, "watching thereunto," more literally, "being sleepless thereunto." Paul realized the natural slothfulness of man, and especially his natural slothfulness in prayer. How seldom we pray things through! How often the church and the individual get right up to the verge of a great blessing in prayer and just then let go, get drowsy, quit. I wish that these words "being sleepless unto prayer" might burn into our hearts. I wish the whole verse might burn into our hearts.

Buy why is this constant, persistent, sleepless, overcoming prayer so needful?

1. First of all, *because there is a devil.*

He is cunning, he is mighty, he never rests, he is ever plotting the downfall of the child of God; and if the child of God relaxes in prayer, the devil will succeed in ensnaring him.

This is the thought of the context. The 12th verse reads: "For our wrestling is not against flesh and blood, but against the principalities, against the powers, against the world rulers of this darkness, against the spiritual hosts of wickedness in the heavenly places." (R. V.) Then comes the 13th verse: "Wherefore take up the whole armor of God, that ye may be able to withstand in the evil day, and, having done all, to stand." (R. V.) Next follows a description of the different parts of the Christian's armor, which we are to put on if we are to stand against the devil and his mighty wiles. Then Paul brings all to a climax in the 18th verse, telling us that to all else we must add prayer — constant, persistent, untiring, sleepless prayer in the Holy Spirit, or all else will go for nothing.

2. A second reason for this constant, persistent, sleepless, overcoming prayer is that *prayer is God's appointed way for obtaining things, and the great secret of all lack in our experience, in our life and in our work is neglect of prayer.*

James brings this out very forcibly in the 4th chapter and 2d verse of his epistle: "Ye have not because ye ask not." These words contain the secret of the poverty and powerlessness of the average Christian — neglect of prayer.

"Why is it," many a Christian is asking, "I make so little progress in my Christian life?"

"Neglect of prayer," God answers. "You have not because you ask not."

"Why is it," many a minister is asking, "I see so little fruit from my labors?"

Again God answers, "Neglect of prayer. You have not because you ask not."

"Why is it," many a Sunday schoolteacher is asking, "that I see so few converted in my Sunday school class?"

Still God answers, "Neglect of prayer. You have not because you ask not."

"Why is it," both ministers and churches are asking, "that the Church of Christ makes so little headway against unbelief and error

THE IMPORTANCE OF PRAYER

and sin and worldliness?"

Once more we hear God answering, "Neglect of prayer. You have not because you ask not."

3. The third reason for this constant, persistent, sleepless, overcoming prayer is that *those men whom God set forth as a pattern of what He expected Christians to be — the apostles — regarded prayer as the most important business of their lives.*

When the multiplying responsibilities of the early church crowded in upon them, they "called the multitude of the disciples unto them, and said, It is not reason that we should leave the Word of God, and serve tables. Wherefore, brethren, look ye out among you seven men of honest report, full of the Holy Ghost and wisdom, whom we may appoint over this business. But *we will give ourselves continually to prayer* and to the ministry of the Word." It is evident from what Paul wrote to the churches and to individuals about praying for them, that very much of his time and strength and thought was given to prayer. (Rom. 1:9, R. V.; Eph. 1:15, 16; Col. 1:9, R. V.; 1 Thess. 3:10; 2 Tim. 1:3, R. V.)

All the mighty men of God outside the Bible have been men of prayer. They have differed from one another in many things, but in this they have been alike.

4. But there is still weightier reason for this constant, persistent, sleepless, overcoming prayer. It is, *prayer occupied a very prominent place and played a very important part in the earthly life of our Lord.*

Turn, for example, to Mark 1:35. We read, "And in the morning, rising up a great while before day, He went out, and departed into a solitary place, and there prayed." The preceding day had been a very busy and exciting one, but Jesus shortened the hours of needed sleep that He might arise early and give Himself to more sorely needed prayer.

Turn again to Luke 6:12, where we read, "And it came to pass in those days that He went out into a mountain to pray, and continued all night in prayer to God." Our Savior found it necessary on occasion to take a whole night for prayer.

The words "pray" and "prayer" are used at least twenty-five times in connection with our Lord in the brief record of His life in the four Gospels, and His praying is mentioned in places where the words are not used. Evidently prayer took much of the time and strength of Jesus, and a man or woman who does not spend much time in prayer, cannot properly be called a follower of Jesus Christ.

5. There is another reason for constant, persistent, sleepless, overcoming prayer that seems if possible even more forcible than this, namely, *praying is the most important part of the present ministry of our risen Lord.*

Christ's ministry did not close with His death. His atoning work was finished then, but when He rose and ascended to the right hand of the Father, He entered upon other work for us just as important in its place as His atoning work. It cannot be divorced from His atoning work; it rests upon that as its basis, but it is necessary to our complete salvation.

What that great present work is, by which He carries our salvation on to completeness, we read in Heb. 7:25, "Wherefore He is able also to save them to the uttermost that come unto God by Him, seeing *He ever liveth to make intercession for them.*" This verse tells us that Jesus is able to save us unto the uttermost, not merely *from* the uttermost, but *unto* the uttermost, unto entire completeness, absolute perfection, because He not merely died, but because He also "ever liveth." The verse also tells us for what purpose He now lives, "*to make intercession* for us," to pray. Praying is the principal thing He is doing in these days. It is by His prayers that He is saving us.

The same thought is found in Paul's remarkable, triumphant challenge in Rom. 8:34 — "Who is he that shall condemn? It is Christ Jesus that died, yea rather, that was raised from the dead, who is at the right hand of God, *who also maketh intercession for us.*" (R. V.)

If we then are to have fellowship with Jesus Christ in His present work, we must spend much time in prayer; we must give ourselves to earnest, constant, persistent, sleepless, overcoming prayer. I know of nothing that has so impressed me with a sense of the importance of praying at all seasons, being much and constantly in prayer, as the thought that that is the principal occupation at present of my risen Lord. I want to have fellowship with Him, and to that end I have asked the Father that whatever else He may make me, to make me at all events an intercessor, to make me a man who knows how to pray, and who spends much time in prayer.

This ministry of intercession is a glorious and a mighty ministry, and we can all have part in it. The man or the woman who is shut away from the public meeting by sickness can have part in it; the busy mother; the woman who has to take in washing for a living can have part — she can mingle prayers for the saints, and for her pastor, and for the unsaved, and for foreign missionaries, with the soap and water as she bends over the washtub, and not do the washing any more poorly on that account; the hard driven man of business can have part in it, praying as he hurries from duty to duty. But of course we must, if we would maintain this spirit of constant prayer, take time — and take plenty of it — when we shall shut ourselves up in the secret place alone with God for nothing but prayer.

6. The sixth reason for constant, persistent, sleepless, overcoming prayer is that *prayer is the means that God has appointed for our receiving mercy, and obtaining grace to help in time of need.*

Heb. 4:16 is one of the simplest and sweetest verses in the Bible — "Let us therefore come boldly unto the throne of grace, that we may obtain mercy, and find grace to help in time of need." These words make it very plain that God has appointed a way by which we shall seek and obtain mercy and grace. That way is prayer; bold, confident, outspoken approach to the throne of grace, the most holy place of God's presence, where our sympathizing High Priest, Jesus Christ, has entered in our behalf. (Verses 14, 15.)

Mercy is what we need, grace is what we must have, or all our life and effort will end in complete failure. Prayer is the way to get them. There is infinite grace at our disposal, and we make it ours experimentally by prayer. Oh, if we only realized the fullness of God's grace that is ours for the asking, its height and depth and length and breadth, I am sure that we would spend more time in prayer. The measure of our appropriation of grace is determined by the measure of our prayers.

Who is there that does not feel that he needs more grace? Then ask for it. Be constant and persistent in your asking. Be importunate and untiring in your asking. God delights to have us "shameless" beggars in this direction; for it shows our faith in Him, and He is mightily pleased with faith. Because of our "shamelessness" He will rise and give us as much as we need (Luke 11:8). What little streams of mercy and grace most of us know, when we might know rivers overflowing their banks!

7. The next reason for constant, persistent, sleepless, overcoming prayer is that *prayer in the name of Jesus Christ is the way Jesus Christ Himself has appointed for His disciples to obtain fullness of joy.*

He states this simply and beautifully in John 16:24, "Hitherto have asked nothing in My name; ask, and ye shall receive, that your joy may be fulfilled." "Made full" is the way the Revised Version reads. Who is there that does not wish his joy filled full? Well, the way to have it filled full is by praying in the name of Jesus. We all know people whose joy is filled full, indeed, it is just running over, is shining from their eyes, bubbling out of their very lips, and running off their fingertips when they shake hands with you. Coming in contact with them is like coming in contact with an electrical machine charged with gladness. Now people of that sort are always people that spend much time in prayer.

Why is it that prayer in the name of Christ brings such fullness of joy? In part, because we get what we ask. But that is not the only reason, nor the greatest. It makes God real. When we ask something definite of God, and He gives it, how real God becomes! He is right there! It is blessed to have a God who is real, and not merely an idea. I remember how once I was taken suddenly and seriously sick all alone in my study. I dropped upon my knees and cried to God for help. Instantly all pain left me — I was perfectly well. It seemed as if God stood right there, and had put out His hand and touched me. The joy of the healing was not so great as the joy of meeting God.

There is no greater joy on earth or in heaven than communion with God, and prayer in the name of Jesus brings us into communion with Him. The Psalmist was surely not speaking only of future blessedness, but also of present blessedness when he said, "In Thy presence is fullness of joy." (Ps. 16:11.) Oh, the unutterable joy of those moments when in our prayers we really press into the presence of God!

Does someone say, "I have never known any such joy as that in prayer"?

Do you take enough leisure for prayer to actually get into God's presence? Do you really give yourself up to prayer in the time which you do take?

8. The eighth reason for constant, persistent, sleepless, overcoming prayer is that *prayer, in every care and anxiety and need of life, with thanksgiving, is the means that God has appointed for our obtaining freedom from all anxiety, and the peace of God which passeth all understanding.*

"Be careful for nothing," says Paul, "but in everything by prayer and supplication with thanksgiving let your requests be made known unto God, and the peace of God which passeth all understanding, shall keep your hearts and minds through Christ Jesus." (Phil. 4:6, 7.) To many this seems, at the first glance, the picture of a life that is beautiful, but beyond the reach of ordinary mortals; not so at all. The verse tells us how the life is attainable by every child of God: "Be careful for nothing," or as the Revised Version reads, "In nothing be anxious." The remainder of the verse tells us how, and it is very simple: "But in everything by prayer and supplication with thanksgiving let your requests be made known unto God." What could be plainer or more simple than that? Just keep in constant touch with God, and when any trouble or vexation, great or small, comes up, speak to Him about it, never forgetting to return thanks for what He has already done. What will the result be? "The peace of God which passeth all understanding shall guard your hearts and your thoughts in Christ Jesus." (R. V.)

That is glorious, and as simple as it is glorious! Thank God, many are trying it. Don't you know anyone who is always serene? Perhaps he is a very stormy man by his natural make-up, but troubles and conflicts and reverses and bereavements may sweep around him, and the peace of God which passeth all understanding guards his heart and his thoughts in Christ Jesus.

We all know such persons. How do they manage it?

Just by prayer, that is all. Those persons who know the deep peace of God, the unfathomable peace that passeth all understanding, are always men and women of much prayer.

Some of us let the hurry of our lives crowd prayer out, and what a waste of time and energy and nerve force there is by the constant worry! One night of prayer will save us from many nights of insomnia. Time spent in prayer is not wasted, but time invested at big interest.

9. The ninth reason for constant, persistent, sleepless, overcoming prayer is that *prayer is the method that God Himself has appointed for our obtaining the Holy Spirit.*

Upon this point the Bible is very plain. Jesus says, "If ye then, being evil, know how to give good gifts unto your children, how much more shall your heavenly Father give the Holy Spirit to them that ask Him?" (Luke 11:13.) Men are telling us in these days, very good men too, "You must not pray for the Holy Spirit," but what are they going to do with the plain statement of Jesus Christ, "How much more will your heavenly Father give the Holy Spirit *to them that ask Him?*"

Some years ago when an address on the baptism with the Holy Spirit was announced, a brother came to me before the address and said with much feeling,

"Be sure and tell them not to pray for the Holy Spirit."

"I will surely not tell them that, for Jesus says, 'How much more shall your heavenly Father give the Holy Spirit to them that ask Him.'"

"Oh yes," he replied, "but that was before Pentecost."

"How about Acts 4:31? was that before Pentecost, or after?"

"After, of course."

"Read it."

"'And when *they had prayed*, the place was shaken where they were assembled together; and they were all *filled with the Holy Ghost*, and they spake the word of God with boldness.'"

"How about Acts 8:15? was that before Pentecost or after?"

"After."

"Please read."

"'Who, when they were come down, *prayed* for them, that they might receive the Holy Ghost.'"

He made no answer. What could he answer? It is plain as day in the Word of God that before Pentecost and after, the first baptism and the subsequent fillings with the Holy Spirit were received in answer to definite prayer. Experience also teaches this.

Doubtless many have received the Holy Spirit the moment of their surrender to God before there was time to pray, but how many there are who know that their first definite baptism with the Holy Spirit came while they were on their knees or faces before God, alone or in company with others, and who again and again since that have been filled with the Holy Spirit in the place of prayer!

I know this as definitely as I know that my thirst has been quenched while I was drinking water. Early one morning in the Chicago Avenue Church prayer room, where several hundred people had been assembled a number of hours in prayer, the Holy Spirit fell so manifestly, and the whole place was so filled with His presence, that no one could speak or pray, but sobs of joy filled the place. Men went out of that room to different parts of the country, taking trains that very morning, and reports soon came back of the outpouring of God's Holy Spirit in answer to prayer. Others went out into the city with the blessing of God upon them. This is only one instance among many that might be cited from personal experience.

THE IMPORTANCE OF PRAYER

If we would only spend more time in prayer, there would be more fullness of the Spirit's power in our work. Many and many a man who once worked unmistakably in the power of the Holy Spirit is now filling the air with empty shoutings, and beating it with his meaningless gesticulations, because he has let prayer be crowded out. We must spend much time on our knees before God, if we are to continue in the power of the Holy Spirit.

10. The tenth reason for constant, persistent, sleepless, overcoming prayer is that *prayer is the means that Christ has appointed whereby our hearts shall not become overcharged with surfeiting and drunkenness and cares of this life, and so the day of Christ's return come upon us suddenly as a snare.*

One of the most interesting and solemn passages upon prayer in the Bible is along this line. (Luke 21:34-36.) "Take heed to yourselves, lest at any time your hearts be overcharged with surfeiting and drunkenness and cares of this life, and so that day come upon you unawares. For as a snare shall it come on all them that dwell on the face of the whole earth. Watch ye therefore, and *pray always*, that ye may be accounted worthy to escape all these things that shall come to pass, and to stand before the Son of man." According to this passage there is only one way in which we can be prepared for the coming of the Lord when He appears, that is, through much prayer.

The coming again of Jesus Christ is a subject that is awakening much interest and much discussion in our day; but it is one thing to be interested in the Lord's return, and to talk about it, and quite another thing to be prepared for it. We live in an atmosphere that has a constant tendency to unfit us for Christ's coming. The world tends to draw us down by its gratifications and by its cares. There is only one way by which we can rise triumphant above these things — by constant watching unto prayer, that is, by sleeplessness unto prayer. "Watch" in this passage is the same strong word used in Eph. 6:18, and "always" the same strong phrase "in every season." The man who spends little time in prayer, who is not steadfast and constant in prayer, will not be ready for the Lord when He comes. But we may be ready. How? Pray! Pray! Pray!

11. There is one more reason for constant, persistent, sleepless, overcoming prayer, and it is a mighty one: *because of what prayer accomplishes*. Much has really been said upon that already, but there is much also that should be added.

(1) Prayer promotes our spiritual growth as almost nothing else, indeed as nothing else but Bible study; and true prayer and true Bible study go hand in hand.

It is through prayer that my sin is brought to light, my most hidden sin. As I kneel before God and pray, "Search me, O God, and know my heart: try me, and know my thoughts: and see if there be any wicked ways in me," (Ps. 139:23, 24), God shoots the penetrating rays of His light into the innermost recesses of my heart, and the sins I never suspected are brought to view. In answer to prayer, God washes me from mine iniquity and cleanses me from my sin (Ps. 51:2). In answer to prayer my eyes are opened to behold wondrous things out of God's Word (Ps. 119:18). In answer to prayer I get wisdom to know God's way (Jas. 1:5) and strength to walk in it. As I meet God in prayer and gaze into His face, I am changed into His own image from glory to glory (2 Cor. 3:18). Each day of true prayer life finds me liker to my glorious Lord.

John Welch, son-in-law to John Knox, was one of the most faithful men of prayer this world ever saw. He counted that day ill-spent in which seven or eight hours were not used alone with God in prayer and the study of His Word. An old man speaking of him after his death said, "He was a type of Christ."

How came he to be so like his Master?

His prayer life explains the mystery.

(2) Prayer brings power into our work.

If we wish power for any work to which God calls us, be it preaching, teaching, personal work, or the rearing of our children, we can get it by earnest prayer.

A woman with a little boy who was perfectly incorrigible, once came to me in desperation and said:

"What shall I do with him?"

I asked, "Have you ever tried prayer?"

She said that she had prayed for him, she thought. I asked if she had made his conversion and his character a matter of definite, expectant prayer. She replied that she had not been definite in the matter. She began that day, and at once there was a marked change in the child, and he grew up into Christian manhood.

How many a Sunday schoolteacher has taught for months and years, and seen no real fruit from his labors, and then has learned the secret of intercession, and by earnest pleading with God, has seen his scholars brought one by one to Christ! How many a poor preacher has become a mighty man of God by casting away his confidence in his own ability and gifts, and giving himself up to God to wait upon Him for the power that comes from on high! John Livingstone spent a night, with some others likeminded, in prayer to God and religious conversation, and when he preached next day in the Kirk of Shotts five hundred people were converted, or dated some definite uplift in their life to that occasion. Prayer and power are inseparable.

(3) Prayer avails from the conversion of others.

There are few converted in this world unless in connection with someone's prayers. I formerly thought that no human being had anything to do with my own conversion, for I was not converted in church or Sunday school, or in personal conversation with anyone. I was awakened in the middle of the night and converted. As far as I can remember I had not the slightest thought of being converted, or of anything of that character, when I went to bed and fell asleep; but I was awakened in the middle of the night and converted probably inside of five minutes. A few minutes before I was about as near eternal perdition as one gets. I had one foot over the brink and was trying to get the other one over. I say I thought no human being had anything to do with it, but I had forgotten my mother's prayers, and I afterward learned that one of my college classmates had chosen me as one to pray for until I was saved.

Prayer often avails where everything else fails. How utterly all of Monica's efforts and entreaties failed with her son, but her prayers prevailed with God, and the dissolute youth became St. Augustine, the mighty man of God. By prayer the bitterest enemies of the Gospel have become its most valiant defenders, the greatest scoundrels the truest sons of God, and the vilest women the purest saints. Oh, the power of prayer to reach down, down, down where hope itself seems vain, and lift men and women up, up, up into fellowship with and likeness to God. It is simply wonderful! How little we appreciate this marvelous weapon!

(4) Prayer brings blessings to the church.

The history of the church has always been a history of grave difficulties to overcome. The devil hates the church and seeks in every way to block its progress; now by false doctrine, again by division, again by inward corruption of life. But by prayer, a clear way can be made through everything. Prayer will root out heresy, allay misunderstanding, sweep away jealousies and animosities, obliterate immoralities, and bring in the full tide of God's reviving grace. History abundantly proves this. In the hour of darkest portent, when the case of the church, local or universal, has seemed beyond hope, believing men and believing women have met together and cried to God and the answer has come.

It was so in the days of Knox, it was so in the days of Wesley and Whitfield, it was so in the days of Edwards and Brainerd, it was so in the days of Finney, it was so in the days of the great revival of 1857 in this country and of 1859 in Ireland, and it will be so again in your day and mine. Satan has marshalled his forces. Christian science with its false Christ — a woman — lifts high its head. Others making great pretentions of apostolic methods, but covering the rankest dishonesty and hypocrisy with these pretentions, speak with loud assurance. Christians equally loyal to the great fundamental truths of the Gospel are glowering at one another with a devil-sent suspicion. The world, the flesh and the devil are holding high carnival. It is now a dark day, *but* — now "it is time for Thee, Lord, to work; for they have made void Thy law." (Ps. 119:126.) And He is getting ready to work, and now He is listening for the voice of prayer. Will He hear it? Will He hear it from you? Will He hear it from the church as a body? I believe He will.

Chapter II
PRAYING UNTO GOD

We have seen something of the tremendous importance and the resistless power of prayer, and now we come directly to the question — how to pray with power.

1. In the 12th chapter of the Acts of the Apostles we have the record of a prayer that prevailed with God, and brought to pass great results. In the 5th verse of this chapter, the manner and method of this prayer is described in few words:

"Prayer was made without ceasing of the church *unto God* for him."

The first thing to notice in this verse is the brief expression "unto God." The prayer that has power is the prayer that is offered unto God.

But some will say, "Is not all prayer unto God?"

No. Very much of so-called prayer, both public and private, is not unto God. In order that a prayer should be really unto God, there must be a definite and conscious approach to God when we pray; we must have a definite and vivid realization that God is bending over us and listening as we pray. In very much of our prayer there is really but little thought of God. Our mind is taken up with the thought of what we need, and is not occupied with the thought of the mighty and loving Father of whom we are seeking it. Oftentimes it is the case that we are occupied neither with the need nor with the One to whom we are praying, but our mind is wandering here and there throughout the world. There is no power in that sort of prayer. But when we really come into God's presence, really meet Him face to face in the place of prayer, really seek the things that we desire *from Him*, then there is power.

If, then, we would pray aright, the first thing that we should do is to see to it that we really get an audience with God, that we really get into His very presence. Before a word of petition is offered, we should have the definite and vivid consciousness that we are talking to God, and should believe that He is listening to our petition and is going to grant the thing that we ask of Him. This is only possible by the Holy Spirit's power, so we should look to the Holy Spirit to really lead us into the presence of God, and should not be hasty in words until He has actually brought us there.

One night a very active Christian man dropped into a little prayer meeting that I was leading. Before we knelt to pray, I said something like the above, telling all the friends to be sure before they prayed, and while they were praying, that they really were in God's presence, that they had the thought of Him definitely in mind, and to be more taken up with Him than with their petition. A few days afterward I met this same gentleman, and he said that this simple thought was entirely new to him, that it had made prayer an entirely new experience to him.

If then we would pray aright, these two little words must sink deep into our hearts, *"unto God."*

2. The second secret of effective praying is found in the same verse, in the words *"without ceasing."*

In the Revised Version, "without ceasing" is rendered "earnestly." Neither rendering gives the full force of the Greek. The word means literally "stretched-out-ed-ly." It is a pictorial word, and wonderfully expressive. It represents the soul on a stretch of earnest and intense desire. "Intensely" would perhaps come as near translating it as any English word. It is the word used of our Lord in Luke 22:44 where it is said, "He prayed more earnestly: and His sweat was as it were great drops of blood falling down to the ground."

We read in Heb. 5:7 that "in the days of His flesh" Christ "offered up prayers and supplications with strong crying and tears." In Rom. 15:30, Paul beseeches the saints in Rome to *strive* together with him in their prayers. The word translated "strive" means primarily to contend as in athletic games or in a fight. In other words, the prayer that prevails with God is the prayer into which we put our whole soul, stretching out toward God in intense and agonizing desire. Much of our modern prayer has no power in it because there is no heart in it. We rush into God's presence, run through a string of petitions, jump up and go out. If someone should ask us an hour afterward for what we prayed, oftentimes we could not tell. If we put so little heart into our prayers, we cannot expect God to put much heart into answering them.

We hear much in our day of the rest of faith, but there is such a thing as the fight of faith in prayer as well as in effort. Those who would have us think that they have attained to some sublime height of faith and trust because they never know any agony of conflict or of prayer, have surely gotten beyond their Lord, and beyond the mightiest victors for God, both in effort and prayer, that the ages of Christian history have known. When we learn to come to God with an intensity of desire that wrings the soul, then shall we know a power in prayer that most of us do not know now.

But how shall we attain to this earnestness in prayer?

Not by trying to work ourselves up into it. The true method is explained in Rom. 8:26, "And in like manner the Spirit also helpeth our infirmity: for we know not how to pray as we ought; but the Spirit Himself maketh intercession for us with groanings which cannot be uttered." (R. V.) The earnestness that we work up in the energy of the flesh is a repulsive thing. The earnestness wrought in us by the power of the Holy Spirit is pleasing to God. Here again, if we would pray aright, we must look to the Spirit of God to teach us to pray.

It is in this connection that fasting comes. In Dan. 9:3 we read that Daniel set his face "unto the Lord God, to seek by prayer and supplications, with fasting, and sackcloth, and ashes." There are those who think that fasting belongs to the old dispensation; but when we look at Acts 14:23, and Acts 13:2, 3, we find that it was practised by the earnest men of the apostolic day.

If we would pray with power, we should pray with fasting. This of course does not mean that we should fast every time we pray; but there are times of emergency or special crisis in work or in our individual lives, when men of downright earnestness will withdraw themselves even from the gratification of natural appetites that would be perfectly proper under other circumstances, that they may give themselves up wholly to prayer. There is a peculiar power in such prayer. Every great crisis in life and work should be met in that way. There is nothing pleasing to God in our giving up in a purely Pharisaic and legal way things which are pleasant, but there is power in that downright earnestness and determination to obtain in prayer the things of which we sorely feel our need, that leads us to put away everything, even things in themselves most right and necessary, that we may set our faces to find God, and obtain blessings from Him.

3. A third secret of right praying is also found in this same verse, Acts

12:5. It appears in the three words *"of the church."*

There is power in *united prayer*. Of course there is power in the prayer of an individual, but there is vastly increased power in united prayer. God delights in the unity of His people, and seeks to emphasize it in every way, and so He pronounces a special blessing upon united prayer. We read in Matt. 18:19, "If two of you shall agree on earth as touching anything that they shall ask, it shall be done for them of My Father which is in heaven." This unity, however, must be real. The passage just quoted does not say that if two shall agree in asking, but if two shall agree *as touching* anything they shall ask. Two persons might agree to ask for the same thing, and yet there be no real agreement as touching the thing they asked. One might ask it because he really desired it, the other might ask it simply to please his friend. But where there is real agreement, where the Spirit of God brings two believers into perfect harmony as concerning that which they may ask of God, where the Spirit lays the same burden on two hearts; in all such prayer there is absolutely irresistible power.

Chapter III
OBEYING AND PRAYING

1. One of the most significant verses in the Bible on prayer is 1 John 3:22. John says, "And whatsoever we ask, we receive of Him, because we keep His commandments, and do those things that are pleasing in His sight."

What an astounding statement! John says, in so many words, that everything he asked for he got. How many of us can say this: "Whatsoever I ask I receive"? But John explains why this was so, "Because we keep His commandments, and do those things that are pleasing in His sight." In other words, the one who expects God to do as he asks Him, must on his part *do whatever God bids him*. If we give a listening ear to all God's commands to us, He will give a listening ear to all our petitions to Him. If, on the other hand, we turn a deaf ear to His precepts, He will be likely to turn a deaf ear to our prayers. Here we find the secret of much unanswered prayer. We are not listening to God's Word, and therefore He is not listening to our petitions.

I was once speaking to a woman who had been a professed Christian, but had given it all up. I asked her why she was not a Christian still. She replied, because she did not believe the Bible. I asked her why she did not believe the Bible.

"Because I have tried its promises and found them untrue."

"Which promises?"

"The promises about prayer."

"Which promises about prayer?"

"Does it not say in the Bible, 'Whatsoever ye ask believing ye shall receive' ?"

"It says something nearly like that."

"Well, I asked fully expecting to get and did not receive, so the promise failed."

"Was the promise made to you?"

"Why, certainly, it is made to all Christians, is it not?"

"No, God carefully defines who the *'ye's'* are, whose believing prayers He agrees to answer."

I then turned her to 1 John 3:22, and read the description of those whose prayers had power with God.

"Now," I said, "were you keeping His commandments and doing those things which are pleasing in His sight?"

She frankly confessed that she was not, and soon came to see that the real difficulty was not with God's promises, but with herself. That is the difficulty with many an unanswered prayer today: the one who offers it is not obedient.

If we would have power in prayer, we must be earnest students of His Word to find out what His will regarding us is, and then having found it, do it. One unconfessed act of disobedience on our part will shut the ear of God against many petitions.

2. But this verse goes beyond the mere keeping of God's commandments. John tells us that we must *do those things that are pleasing in His sight*.

There are many things which it would be pleasing to God for us to do which He has not specifically commanded us. A true child is not content with merely doing those things which his father specifically commands him to do. He studies to know his father's will, and if he thinks that there is anything that he can do that would please his father, he does it gladly, though his father has never given him any specific order to do it. So it is with the true child of God. He does not ask merely whether certain things are commanded or certain things forbidden. He studies to know his Father's will in all things.

There are many Christians today who are doing things that are not pleasing to God, and leaving undone things which would be pleasing to God. When you speak to them about these things they will confront you at once with the question, "Is there any command in the Bible not to do this thing?" And if you cannot show them some verse in which the matter in question is plainly forbidden, they think they are under no obligation whatever to give it up; but a true child of God does not demand a specific command. If we make it our study to find out and to do the things which are pleasing to God, He will make it His study to do the things which are pleasing to us. Here again we find the explanation of much unanswered prayer: We are not making it the study of our lives to know what would please our Father, and so our prayers are not answered.

Take as an illustration of questions that are constantly coming up, the matter of theater going, dancing and the use of tobacco. Many who are indulging in these things will ask you triumphantly if you speak against them, "Does the Bible say, 'Thou shalt not go to the theater'?" "Does the Bible say, 'Thou shalt not dance'?" "Does the Bible say, 'Thou shalt not smoke'?" That is not the question. The question is, Is our heavenly Father well pleased when He sees one of His children in the theater, at the dance, or smoking? That is a question for each to decide for himself, prayerfully, seeking light from the Holy Spirit. "Where is the harm in these things?" many ask. It is aside from our purpose to go into the general question, but beyond a doubt there is this great harm in many a case; they rob our prayers of power.

3. Psalm 145:18 throws a great deal of light on the question of how to pray: "The Lord is nigh unto all them that call upon Him, to all that call upon Him in truth."

That little expression "in truth" is worthy of study. If you will take your concordance and go through the Bible, you will find that this expression means "in reality," "in sincerity." The prayer that God answers is the prayer that is real, the prayer that asks for something that is sincerely desired.

Much prayer is insincere. People ask for things which they do not wish. Many a woman is praying for the conversion of her husband, who does not really wish her husband to be converted. She thinks that she does, but if she knew what would be involved in the conversion of her husband, how it would necessitate an entire revolution in his manner of doing business, and how consequently it would reduce their income and make necessary an entire change in their method of living, the real prayer of her heart would be, if she were to be sincere with God:

"Oh God, do not convert my husband."

She does not wish his conversion at so great cost.

Many a church is praying for a revival that does not really desire a revival. They think they do, for to their minds a revival means an increase of membership, an increase of income, an increase of reputation among the churches; but if they knew what a real revival meant, what a searching of hearts on the part of professed Christians would be involved, what a radical transformation of individual, domestic and social life would be brought about, and many other things that would come to pass if the Spirit of God was poured out in reality and power; if all this were known, the real cry of the church would be:

"Oh God, keep us from having a revival."

Many a minister is praying for the baptism with the Holy Spirit who does not really desire it. He thinks he does, for the baptism with the Spirit means to him new joy, new power in preaching the Word, a wider reputation among men, a larger prominence in the church of Christ. But if he understood what a baptism with the Holy Spirit really involved, how for example it would necessarily bring him into antagonism with the world, and with unspiritual Christians, how it would cause his name to be "cast out as evil," how it might necessitate his leaving a good comfortable living and going down to work in the slums, or even in some foreign land; if he understood all this, his prayer quite likely would be — if he were to express the real wish of his heart —

"Oh God, save me from being baptized with the Holy Ghost."

But when we do come to the place where we really desire the conversion of friends at any cost, really desire the outpouring of the Holy Spirit whatever it may involve, really desire the baptism with the Holy Ghost come what may, where we desire anything "in truth" and then call upon God for it "in truth," God is going to hear.

Chapter IV
PRAYING IN THE NAME OF CHRIST AND ACCORDING TO THE WILL OF GOD

1. It was a wonderful word about prayer that Jesus spoke to His disciples on the night before His crucifixion, "Whatsoever ye shall ask *in My name*, that will I do, that the Father may be glorified in the Son. If ye shall ask anything in My name, I will do it."

Prayer in the name of Christ has power with God. God is well pleased with His Son Jesus Christ. He hears Him always, and He also hears always the prayer that is really in His name. There is a fragrance in the name of Christ that makes acceptable to God every prayer that bears it.

But what is it to pray in the name of Christ?

Many explanations have been attempted that to ordinary minds do not explain. But there is nothing mystical or mysterious about this expression. If one will go through the Bible and examine all the passages in which the expression "in My name" or "in His name" or synonymous expressions are used, he will find that it means just about what it does in modern usage. If I go to a bank and hand in a check with my name signed to it, I ask of that bank *in my own name*. If I have money deposited in that bank, the check will be cashed; if not, it will not be. If, however, I go to a bank with somebody else's name signed to the check, I am asking *in his name*, and it does not matter whether I have money in that bank or any other, if the person whose name is signed to the check has money there, the check will be cashed.

If, for example, I should go to the First National Bank of Chicago, and present a check which I had signed for $50.00, the paying teller would say to me:

"Why, Mr. Torrey, we cannot cash that. You have no money in this bank."

But if I should go to the First National Bank with a check for $5,000.00 made payable to me, and signed by one of the large depositors in that bank, they would not ask whether I had money in that bank or in any bank, but would honor the check at once.

So it is when I go to the bank of heaven, when I go to God in prayer. I have nothing deposited there, I have absolutely no credit there, and if I go in my own name I will get absolutely nothing; but Jesus Christ has unlimited credit in heaven, and He has granted to me the privilege of going to the bank with His name on my checks, and when I thus go, my prayers will be honored to any extent.

To pray then in the name of Christ is to pray on the ground, not of my credit, but His; to renounce the thought that I have any claims on God whatever, and approach Him on the ground of Christ's claims. Praying in the name of Christ is not merely adding the phrase "I ask these things in Jesus' name" to my prayer. I may put that phrase in my prayer and really be resting in my own merit all the time. On the other hand, I may omit that phrase but really be resting in the merit of Christ all the time. But when I really do approach God, not on the ground of my merit, but on the ground of Christ's merit, not on the ground of my goodness, but on the ground of the atoning blood (Heb. 10:19), God will hear me. Very much of our modern prayer is vain because men approach God imagining that they have some claim upon God whereby He is under obligations to answer their prayers.

Years ago when Mr. Moody was young in Christian work, he visited a town in Illinois. A judge in the town was an infidel. This judge's wife besought Mr. Moody to call upon her husband, but Mr. Moody replied:

"I cannot talk with your husband. I am only an uneducated young Christian, and your husband is a book infidel."

But the wife would not take no for an answer, so Mr. Moody made the call. The clerks in the outer office tittered as the young salesman from Chicago went in to talk with the scholarly judge.

The conversation was short. Mr. Moody said:

"Judge, I can't talk with you. You are a book infidel, and I have no learning, but I simply want to say if you are ever converted, I want you to let me know."

The judge replied: "Yes, young man, if I am ever converted I will let you know. Yes, I will let you know."

The conversation ended. The clerks tittered still louder when the zealous young Christian left the office, but the judge was converted within a year. Mr. Moody visiting the town again asked the judge to explain how it came about. The judge said:

"One night, when my wife was at prayer meeting, I began to grow very uneasy and miserable. I did not know what was the matter with me, but finally retired before my wife came home. I could not sleep all that night. I got up early, told my wife that I would eat no breakfast, and went down to the office. I told the clerks they could take a holiday, and shut myself up in the inner office. I kept growing more and more miserable, and finally I got down and asked God to forgive my sins, but I would not say 'for Jesus' sake,' for I was a Unitarian and I did not believe in atonement. I kept praying 'God forgive my sins'; but no answer came. At last in desperation I cried, 'Oh God, for Christ's sake forgive my sins,' and found peace at once."

The judge had no access to God until he came in the name of Christ, but when he thus came, he was heard and answered at once.

2. Great light is thrown upon the subject "How to Pray" by 1 John 5:14, 15: "And this is the boldness which we have toward Him, that if we ask anything *according to His Will*, He heareth us: and if we know that He heareth us whatsoever we ask, we know that we have the petitions which we have asked of Him." (R. V.)

This passage teaches us plainly that if we are to pray aright, we must pray according to God's will, then will we beyond a peradventure get the thing we ask of Him.

But can we know the will of God? Can we know that any specific prayer is according to His will?

We most surely can.

How?

(1) First by the Word. God has revealed His will in His Word. When anything is definitely promised in the Word of God, we know that it is His will to give that thing. If then when I pray, I can find some definite promise of God's Word and lay that promise before God, I know that He hears me, and if I know that He hears me, I know that I have the petition that I have asked of Him. For example, when I pray for wisdom I know that it is the will of God to give me wisdom, for He says so in James 1:5: "If any of you lack wisdom, let him ask of God, that giveth to all men liberally, and upbraideth not; and it shall be given him." So when I ask for wisdom I know that the prayer is heard, and that wisdom will be given me. In like manner when I pray for the Holy

Spirit I know from Luke 11:13 that it is God's will, that my prayer is heard, and that I have the petition that I have asked of Him: "If ye then, being evil, know how to give good gifts unto your children, how much more shall your heavenly Father give the Holy Spirit to them that ask Him?"

Some years ago a minister came to me at the close of an address on prayer at a Y.M.C.A. Bible school, and said,

"You have produced upon those young men the impression that they can ask for definite things and get the very things that they ask."

I replied that I did not know whether that was the impression that I produced or not, but that was certainly the impression that I desired to produce.

"But," he replied, "that is not right. We cannot be sure, for we don't know God's will."

I turned him at once to James 1:5, read it and said to him, "Is it not God's will to give us wisdom, and if you ask for wisdom do you not know that you are going to get it?"

"Ah!" he said, "we don't know what wisdom is."

I said, "No, if we did, we would not need to ask; but whatever wisdom may be, don't you know that you will get it?"

Certainly it is our privilege to know. When we have a specific promise in the Word of God, if we doubt that it is God's will, or if we doubt that God will do the thing that we ask, we make God a liar.

Here is one of the greatest secrets of prevailing prayer: To study the Word to find what God's will is as revealed there in the promises, and then simply take these promises and spread them out before God in prayer with the absolutely unwavering expectation that He will do what He has promised in His word.

(2) But there is still another way in which we may know the will of God, that is, by the teaching of His Holy Spirit. There are many things that we need from God which are not covered by any specific promise, but we are not left in ignorance of the will of God even then. In Rom. 8:26, 27 we are told, "And in like manner the Spirit also helpeth our infirmity: for we know not how to pray as we ought; but the Spirit Himself maketh intercession for us with groanings which cannot be uttered; and He that searcheth the hearts knoweth what is the mind of the Spirit, because He maketh intercession for the saints *according to the will of God.*" (R. V.) Here we are distinctly told that the Spirit of God

prays in us, draws out our prayer, in the line of God's will. When we are thus led out by the Holy Spirit in any direction, to pray for any given object, we may do it in all confidence that it is God's will, and that we are to get the very thing we ask of Him, even though there is no specific promise to cover the case. Often God by His Spirit lays upon us a heavy burden of prayer for some given individual. We cannot rest, we pray for him with groanings which cannot be uttered. Perhaps the man is entirely beyond our reach, but God hears the prayer, and in many a case it is not long before we hear of his definite conversion.

The passage 1 John 5:14, 15 is one of the most abused passages in the Bible: "This is *the confidence* that we have in Him, that, if we ask anything according to His will, He heareth us; and if we know that He hear us, whatsoever we ask, we know that we have the petitions that we desired of Him." The Holy Spirit beyond a doubt put it into the Bible to encourage our faith. It begins with "This is *the confidence* that we have in Him," and closes with "*We know* that we have the petitions that we desired of Him"; but one of the most frequent usages of this passage, which was so manifestly given to beget confidence, is to introduce an element of uncertainty into our prayers. Oftentimes when one waxes confident in prayer, some cautious brother will come and say:

"Now, don't be too confident. If it is God's will He will do it. You should put in, 'If it be Thy will.' "

Doubtless there are many times when we do not know the will of God, and in all prayer submission to the excellent will of God should underlie it; but when we know God's will, there need be no "ifs"; and this passage was not put into the Bible in order that we might introduce "ifs" into all our prayers, but in order that we might throw our "ifs" to the wind, and have *"confidence"* and *"know* that we have the petitions which we have asked of Him."

Chapter V
PRAYING IN THE SPIRIT

1. Over and over again in what has already been said, we have seen our dependence upon the Holy Spirit in prayer. This comes out very definitely in Eph. 6:18, "Praying always with all prayer and supplication *in the Spirit,*" and in Jude 20, "Praying *in the Holy Ghost.*" Indeed the whole secret of prayer is found in these three words, "in the Spirit." It is the prayer that God the Holy Spirit inspires that God the Father answers.

The disciples did not know how to pray as they ought, so they came to Jesus and said, "Lord teach us to pray." We know not how to pray as we ought, but we have another Teacher and Guide right at hand to help us (John 14:16, 17), "The Spirit helpeth our infirmity" (Rom. 8:26, R. V.). He teaches us how to pray. True prayer is prayer in the Spirit; that is, the prayer the Spirit inspires and directs. When we come into God's presence we should recognize "our infirmity," our ignorance of what we should pray for or how we should pray for it, and in the consciousness of our utter inability to pray aright we should look up to the Holy Spirit, casting ourselves utterly upon Him to direct our prayers, to lead out our desires and to guide our utterance of them.

Nothing can be more foolish in prayer than to rush heedlessly into God's presence, and ask the first thing that comes into our mind, or that some thoughtless friend has asked us to pray for. When we first come into God's presence we should be silent before Him. We should look up to Him to send His Holy Spirit to teach us how to pray. We must wait for the Holy Spirit, and surrender ourselves to the Spirit, then we shall pray aright.

Oftentimes when we come to God in prayer, we do not feel like praying. What shall one do in such a case? cease praying until he does feel like it? Not at all. When we feel least like praying is the time when we most need to pray. We should wait quietly before God and tell Him how cold and prayerless our hearts are, and look up to Him and trust Him and expect Him to send the Holy Spirit to warm our hearts and draw them out in prayer. It will not be long before the glow of the Spirit's presence will fill our hearts, and we will begin to pray with freedom, directness, earnestness, and power. Many of the most blessed seasons of prayer I have ever known have begun with a feeling of utter deadness and prayerlessness; but in my helplessness and coldness I have cast myself upon God, and looked to Him to send His Holy Spirit to teach me to pray, and He has done it.

When we pray in the Spirit, we will pray for the right things and in the right way. There will be joy and power in our prayer.

2. If we are to pray with power we must pray *with faith*. In Mark 11:24 Jesus says, "Therefore I say unto you, What things soever ye desire, when ye pray, believe that ye receive them, and ye shall have them." No matter how positive any promise of God's Word may be, we will not enjoy it in actual experience unless we confidently expect its fulfillment in answer to our prayer. "If any of you lack wisdom," says James, "let him ask of God that giveth to all men liberally, and upbraideth not; and it shall be given him." Now that promise is as positive as a promise can be, but the next verse adds, "But let him ask in faith, nothing doubting: for he that doubteth is like the surge of the sea driven by the wind and tossed. For let not that man think that he shall receive anything of the Lord." (R. V.) There must then be confident unwavering expectation. But there is a faith that goes beyond expectation, that believes that the prayer is heard and the promise granted. This comes out in the Revised Version of Mark 11:24, "Therefore I say unto you, All things whatsoever ye pray and ask for, believe that ye *have* received them, and ye shall have them."

But how can one get this faith?

Let us say with all emphasis, it cannot be pumped up. Many a one reads this promise about the prayer of faith, and then asks for things that he desires and tries to make himself believe that God has heard the prayer. This ends only in disappointment, for it is not real faith and the thing is not granted. It is at this point that many people make a collapse of faith altogether by trying to work up faith by an effort of their will, and as the thing they made themselves believe they expected to get is not given, the very foundation of faith is oftentimes undermined.

But how does real faith come?

Rom. 10:17 answers the question: "So then faith cometh by hearing, and hearing *by the Word of God.*" If we are to have real faith, we must study the Word of God and find out what is promised, then simply believe the promises of God. Faith must have a warrant. Trying to believe something that you want to believe is not faith. Believing what God says in His Word is faith. If I am to have faith when I pray, I must find some promise in the Word of God on which to rest my faith. Faith furthermore comes through the Spirit. The Spirit knows the will of God, and if I pray in the Spirit, and look to the Spirit to teach me God's will, He will lead me out in prayer along the line of that will, and give me faith that the prayer is to be answered; but in no case does real faith come by simply determining that you are going to get the thing that you want to get. If there is no promise in the Word of God, and no clear leading of the Spirit, there can be no real faith, and there should be no upbraiding of self for lack of faith in such a case. But if the thing desired is promised in the Word of God, we may well upbraid ourselves for lack of faith if we doubt; for we are making God a liar by doubting His Word.

Chapter VI
ALWAYS PRAYING AND NOT FAINTING

In two parables in the Gospel of Luke, Jesus teaches with great emphasis the lesson that men ought always to pray and not to faint. The first parable is found in Luke 11:5-8, and the other in Luke 18:1-8.

"And He said unto them, Which of you shall have a friend, and shall go unto him at midnight, and say unto him: 'Friend, lend me three loaves; for a friend of mine in his journey is come to me, and I have nothing to set before him?' And he from within shall answer and say: 'Trouble me not: the door is now shut, and my children are with me in bed. I cannot rise and give thee.' I say unto you, Though he will not rise and give him because he is his friend, yet because of his importunity he will rise and give him as many as he needeth." (Luke 11:5-8.)

"And He spake a parable unto them to this end, that men always ought to pray and not to faint, saying: 'There was in a city a judge which feared not God, neither regarded man; and there was a widow in that city; and she came to him, saying:

" 'Avenge me of mine adversary.'

"And he would not for a while; but afterward he said within himself: 'Though I fear not God, nor regard man, yet because this widow troubleth me I will avenge her, lest by her continual coming she weary me.'

"And the Lord said, Hear what the unjust judge saith. And shall not God avenge His own elect, which cry day and night unto Him, though He bear long with them? I tell you that He will avenge them speedily. Nevertheless when the Son of man cometh, shall He find faith on the earth?" (Luke 18:1-8.)

In the former of these two parables Jesus sets forth the necessity of importunity in praying in a startling way. The word rendered "importunity" means literally "shamelessness," as if Jesus would have us understand that God would have us draw nigh to Him with a determination to obtain the things we seek that will not be put to shame by any seeming refusal or delay on God's part. God delights in the holy boldness that will not take "no" for an answer. It is an expression of great faith, and nothing pleases God more than faith.

Jesus seemed to put the Syro-Phoenician woman away almost with rudeness, but she would not be put away, and Jesus looked upon her shameless importunity with pleasure, and said, "O woman, great is thy faith: be it unto thee even as thou wilt." (Matt. 15:28.) God does not always let us get things at our first effort. He would train us and make us strong men by compelling us to work hard for the best things. So also He does not always give us what we ask in answer to the first prayer; He would train us and make us strong men of prayer by compelling us to pray hard for the best things. He makes us *pray through*.

I am glad that this is so. There is no more blessed training in prayer than that that comes through being compelled to ask again and again and again even through a long period of years before one obtains that which he seeks from God. Many people call it submission to the will of God when God does not grant them their requests at the first or second asking, and they say:

"Well, perhaps it is not God's will."

As a rule this is not submission, but spiritual laziness. We do not call it submission to the will of God when we give up after one or two efforts to obtain things by action; we call it lack of strength of character. When the strong man of action starts out to accomplish a thing, if he does not accomplish in the first, or second or one hundredth time, he keeps hammering away until he does accomplish it; and the strong man of prayer when he starts to pray for a thing keeps on praying until he prays it through, and obtains what he seeks. We should be careful about what we ask from God, but when we do begin to pray for a thing we should never give up praying for it until we get it, or until God makes it very clear and very definite to us that it is not His will to give it.

Some would have us believe that it shows unbelief to pray twice for the same thing, that we ought to "take it" the first time that we ask. Doubtless there are times when we are able through faith in the Word or the leading of the Holy Spirit to *claim* the first time that which we have asked of God; but beyond question there are other times when we must pray again and again and again for the same thing before we get our answer. Those who have gotten beyond praying twice for the same thing have gotten beyond their Master (Matt. 26:44). George Muller prayed for two men daily for upwards of sixty years. One of these men was converted shortly before his death, I think at the last service that George Muller held, the other was converted within a year after his death. One of the great needs of the present day is men and women who will not only start out to pray for things, but pray on and on and on until they obtain that which they seek from the Lord.

Chapter VII
ABIDING IN CHRIST

"If ye abide in Me, and My words abide in you, ye shall ask what ye will, and it shall be done unto you." (John 15:7.) The whole secret of prayer is found in these words of our Lord. Here is prayer that has unbounded power: "Ask *What ye will,* and it shall be done unto you."

There is a way then of asking and getting precisely what we ask and getting all we ask. Christ gives two conditions of this all-prevailing prayer:

1. The first condition is, "If ye abide in Me."

What is it to abide in Christ?

Some explanations that have been given of this are so mystical or so profound that to many simple-minded children of God they mean practically nothing at all; but what Jesus meant was really very simple.

He had been comparing Himself to a vine, His disciples to the branches in the vine. Some branches continued in the vine, that is, remained in living union with the vine, so that the sap or life of the vine constantly flowed into these branches. They had no independent life of their own. Everything in them was simply the outcome of the life of the vine flowing into them. Their buds, their leaves, their blossoms, their fruit, were really not theirs, but the buds, leaves, blossoms and fruit of the vine. Other branches were completely severed from the vine, or else the flow of the sap or life of the vine into them was in some way hindered. Now for us to abide in Christ is for us to bear the same relation to Him that the first sort of branches bear to the vine; that is to say, to abide in Christ is to renounce any independent life of our own, to give up trying to think our thoughts, or form our resolutions, or cultivate our feelings, and simply and constantly look to Christ to think His thoughts in us, to form His purposes in us, to feel His emotions and affections in us. It is to renounce all life independent of Christ, and constantly to look to Him for the inflow of His life into us, and the outworking of His life through us. When we do this, and insofar as we do this, our prayers will obtain that which we seek from God.

This must necessarily be so, for our desires will not be our own desires, but Christ's, and our prayers will not in reality be our own prayers, but Christ praying in us. Such prayers will always be in harmony with God's will, and the Father heareth Him always. When our prayers fail it is because they are indeed our prayers. We have conceived the desire and framed the petition of ourselves, instead of looking to Christ to pray through us.

To say that one should be abiding in Christ in all his prayers, looking to Christ to pray through Him rather than praying himself, is simply saying in another way that one should pray "in the Spirit." When we thus abide in Christ, our thoughts are not our own thoughts, but His, our joys are not our own joys, but His, our fruit is not our own fruit, but His; just as the buds, leaves, blossoms and fruit of the branch that abides in the vine are not the buds, leaves, blossoms and fruit of the branch, but of the vine itself whose life is flowing into the branch and manifests itself in these buds, leaves, blossoms and fruit.

To abide in Christ, one must of course already be in Christ through the acceptance of Christ as an atoning Savior from the guilt of sin, a risen Savior from the power of sin, and a Lord and Master over all his life. Being in Christ, all that we have to do to abide (or continue) in Christ is simply to renounce our self-life — utterly renouncing every thought, every purpose, every desire, every affection of our own, and just looking day by day and hour by hour for Jesus Christ to form His thoughts, His purposes, His affections, His desires in us. Abiding in Christ is really a very simple matter, though it is a wonderful life of privilege and of power.

2. But there is another condition stated in this verse, though it is really involved in the first: "And My words abide in you."

If we are to obtain from God all that we ask from Him, Christ's words must abide or continue in us. We must study His words, fairly devour His words, let them sink into our thought and into our heart, keep them in our memory, obey them constantly in our life, let them shape and mold our daily life and our every act.

This is really the method of abiding in Christ. It is through His words that Jesus imparts Himself to us. The words He speaks unto us, they are spirit and they are life (John 6:63). It is vain to expect power in prayer unless we meditate much upon the words of Christ, and let them sink deep and find a permanent abode in our hearts. There are many who wonder why they are so powerless in prayer, but the very simple explanation of it all is found in their neglect of the words of Christ. They have not hidden His words in their hearts; His words do not abide in them. It is not by seasons of mystical meditation and rapturous experiences that we learn to abide in Christ; it is by feeding upon His word, His written word as found in the Bible, and looking to the Holy Spirit to implant these words in our hearts and to make them a living thing in our hearts. If we thus let the words of Christ abide in us, they will stir us up to prayer. They will be the mold in which our prayers are shaped, and our prayers will be necessarily along the line of God's will, and will prevail with Him. Prevailing prayer is almost an impossibility where there is neglect of the study of the Word of God.

Mere intellectual study of the Word of God is not enough; there must be meditation upon it. The Word of God must be revolved over and over and over in the mind, with a constant looking to God by His Spirit to make that Word a living thing in the heart. The prayer that is born of meditation upon the Word of God is the prayer that soars upward most easily to God's listening ear.

George Muller, one of the mightiest men of prayer of the past generations, when the hour for prayer came would begin by reading and meditating upon God's Word until out of the study of the Word a prayer began to form itself in his heart. Thus God Himself was the real author of the prayer, and God answered the prayers which He Himself had inspired.

The Word of God is the instrument through which the Holy Spirit works, it is the sword of the Spirit in more senses than one; and the one who would know the work of the Holy Spirit in any direction must feed upon the Word. The one who would pray in the Spirit must meditate much upon the Word, that the Holy Spirit may have something through which He can work. The Holy Spirit works His prayers in us through the Word, and neglect of the Word makes praying in the Holy Spirit an impossibility. If we would feed the fire of our prayers with the fuel of God's Word, all our difficulties in prayer would disappear.

Chapter VIII
PRAYING WITH THANKSGIVING

There are two words often overlooked in the lesson about prayer which Paul gives us in Phil. 4:6, 7, "In nothing be anxious; but in everything by prayer and supplication with thanksgiving let your requests be made known unto God. And the peace of God, which passeth all understanding, shall guard your hearts and your thoughts in Christ Jesus." (R. V.) The two important words often overlooked are, *"with thanksgiving."*

In approaching God to ask for new blessings, we should never forget to return thanks for blessings already granted. If any one of us would stop and think how many of the prayers which we have offered to God have been answered, and how seldom we have gone back to God to return thanks for the answers thus given, I am sure we would be overwhelmed with confusion. We should be just as definite in returning thanks as we are in prayer. We come to God with most specific petitions, but when we return thanks to Him, our thanksgiving is indefinite and general.

Doubtless one reason why so many of our prayers lack power is because we have neglected to return thanks for blessings already received. If anyone were to constantly come to us asking help from us, and should never say "Thank you" for the help thus given, we would soon tire of helping one so ungrateful. Indeed, regard for the one we were helping would hold us back from encouraging such rank ingratitude. Doubtless our heavenly Father out of a wise regard for our highest welfare oftentimes refuses to answer petitions that we send up to Him in order that we may be brought to a sense of our ingratitude and taught to be thankful.

God is deeply grieved by the thanklessness and ingratitude of which so many of us are guilty. When Jesus healed the ten lepers and only one came back to give Him thanks, in wonderment and pain He exclaimed,

"Were not the ten cleansed? but where are the nine?" (Luke 17:17, R. V.)

How often must He look down upon us in sadness at our forgetfulness of His repeated blessings, and His frequent answer to our prayers.

Returning thanks for blessings already received increases our faith and enables us to approach God with new boldness and new assurance. Doubtless the reason so many have so little faith when they pray, is because they take so little time to meditate upon and thank God for blessings already received. As one meditates upon the answers to prayers already granted, faith waxes bolder and bolder, and we come to feel in the very depths of our souls that there is nothing too hard for the Lord. As we reflect upon the wondrous goodness of God toward us on the one hand, and upon the other hand upon the little thought and strength and time that we ever put into thanksgiving, we may well humble ourselves before God and confess our sin.

The mighty men of prayer in the Bible, and the mighty men of prayer throughout the ages of the church's history have been men who were much given to thanksgiving and praise. David was a mighty man of prayer, and how his Psalms abound with thanksgiving and praise. The apostles were mighty men of prayer; of them we read that "they are continually in the temple, praising and blessing God." Paul was a mighty man of prayer, and how often in his epistles he bursts out in definite thanksgiving to God for definite blessings and definite answers to prayers. Jesus is our model in prayer as in everything else. We find in the study of His life that His manner of returning thanks at the simplest meal was so noticeable that two of His disciples recognized Him by this after His resurrection.

Thanksgiving is one of the inevitable results of being filled with the Holy Spirit and one who does not learn "in everything to give thanks" cannot continue to pray in the Spirit. If we would learn to pray with power we would do well to let these two words sink deep into our hearts: "WITH THANKSGIVING."

Chapter IX
HINDRANCES TO PRAYER

We have gone very carefully into the positive conditions of prevailing prayer; but there are some things which hinder prayer. These God has made very plain in His Word.

1. The first hindrance to prayer we will find in James 4:3, "Ye ask and receive not *because ye ask amiss, that ye may spend it in your pleasures.*" (R. V.)

A selfish purpose in prayer robs prayer of power. Very many prayers are selfish. These may be prayers for things for which it is perfectly proper to ask, for things which it is the will of God to give, but the motive of the prayer is entirely wrong, and so the prayer falls powerless to the ground. The true purpose in prayer is that God may be glorified in the answer. If we ask any petition merely that we may receive something to use in our pleasures or in our own gratification in one way or another, we "ask amiss" and need not expect to receive what we ask. This explains why many prayers remain unanswered.

For example, many a woman is praying for the conversion of her husband. That certainly is a most proper thing to ask; but many a woman's motive in asking for the conversion of her husband is entirely improper, it is selfish. She desires that her husband may be converted because it would be so much more pleasant for her to have a husband who sympathized with her; or it is so painful to think that her husband might die and be lost forever. For some such selfish reason as this she desires to have her husband converted. The prayer is purely selfish. Why should a woman desire the conversion of her husband? First of and above all, that God may be glorified; because she cannot bear the thought that God the Father should be dishonored by her husband trampling underfoot the Son of God.

Many pray for a revival. That certainly is a prayer that is pleasing to God, it is along the line of His will; but many prayers for revivals are purely selfish. The churches desire revivals in order that the membership may be increased, in order that the church may have a position of more power and influence in the community, in order that the church treasury may be filled, in order that a good report may be made at the presbytery or conference or association. For such low purposes as these, churches and ministers oftentimes are praying for a revival, and oftentimes too God does not answer the prayer. Why should we pray for a revival? For the glory of God, because we cannot endure it that God should continue to be dishonored by the worldliness of the church, by the sins of unbelievers, by the proud unbelief of the day; because God's Word is being made void; in order that God may be glorified by the outpouring of His Spirit on the Church of Christ. For these reasons first of all and above all, we should pray for a revival.

Many a prayer for the Holy Spirit is a purely selfish prayer. It certainly is God's will to give the Holy Spirit to them that ask Him — He has told us so plainly in His Word (Luke 11:13), but many a prayer for the Holy Spirit is hindered by the selfishness of the motive that lies back of the prayer. Men and women pray for the Holy Spirit in order that they may be happy, or in order that they may be saved from the wretchedness of defeat in their lives, or in order that they may have power as Christian workers, or for some other purely selfish motive. Why should we pray for the Spirit? In order that God may no longer be dishonored by the low level of our Christian lives and by our ineffectiveness in service, in order that God may be glorified in the new beauty that comes into our lives and the new power that comes into our service.

2. The second hindrance to prayer we find is Is. 59:1, 2: "Behold, the Lord's hand is not shortened, that it cannot save; neither His ear heavy, that it cannot hear. But *your iniquities have separated between you and your God, and your sins have hid His face from you, that He will not hear.*"

Sin hinders prayer. Many a man prays and prays and prays, and gets absolutely no answer to his prayer. Perhaps he is tempted to think that it is not the will of God to answer, or he may think that the days when God answered prayer, if He ever did, are over. So the Israelites seem to have thought. They thought that the Lord's hand was shortened, that it could not save, and that His ear had become heavy, that it could no longer hear.

"Not so," said Isaiah, "God's ear is just as open to hear as ever, His

HINDRANCES TO PRAYER

hand just as mighty to save; but there is a hindrance. That hindrance is your own sins. Your iniquities have separated between you and your God, and your sins have hid His face from you that He will not hear."

It is so today. Many and many a man is crying to God in vain, simply because of sin in his life. It may be some sin in the past that has been unconfessed and unjudged, it may be some sin in the present that is cherished, very likely is not even looked upon as sin, but there the sin is, hidden away somewhere in the heart or in the life, and God "will not hear."

Anyone who finds his prayers ineffective should not conclude that the thing which he asks of God is not according to His will, but should go alone with God with the Psalmist's prayer, "Search me, O God, and know my heart: try me, and know my thoughts: and see if there be any wicked way in me" (Ps. 139:23, 24), and wait before Him until He puts His finger upon the thing that is displeasing in His sight. Then this sin should be confessed and put away.

I well remember a time in my life when I was praying for two definite things that it seemed that I must have, or God would be dishonored; but the answer did not come. I awoke in the middle of the night in great physical suffering and great distress of soul. I cried to God for these things, reasoned with Him as to how necessary it was that I get them, and get them at once; but no answer came. I asked God to show me if there was anything wrong in my own life. Something came to my mind that had often come to it before, something definite but which I was unwilling to confess as sin. I said to God, "If this is wrong I will give it up"; but still no answer came. In my innermost heart, though I had never admitted it, I knew it was wrong.

At last I said:

"This is wrong. I have sinned. I will give it up."

I found peace. In a few moments I was sleeping like a child. In the morning I woke well in body, and the money that was so much needed for the honor of God's name came.

Sin is an awful thing, and one of the most awful things about it is the way it hinders prayer, the way it severs the connection between us and the source of all grace and power and blessing. Anyone who would have power in prayer must be merciless in dealing with his own sins. "If I regard iniquity in my heart, the Lord will not hear me." (Ps. 66:18.) So long as we hold onto sin or have any controversy with God, we cannot expect Him to heed our prayers. If there is anything that is constantly coming up in your moments of close communion with God, that is the thing that hinders prayer: put it away.

3. The third hindrance to prayer is found in Ez. 14:3, "Son of man, these men have taken their idols into their heart, and put the stumbling block of their iniquity before their face: should I be inquired of at all by them?" (R. V.) *Idols in the heart cause God to refuse to listen to our prayers.*

What is an idol? An idol is anything that takes the place of God, anything that is the supreme object of our affection. God alone has the right to the supreme place in our hearts. Everything and everyone else must be subordinate to Him.

Many a man makes an idol of his wife. Not that a man can love his wife any too much, but he can put her in the wrong place, he can put her before God; and when a man regards his wife's pleasure before God's pleasure, when he gives her the first place and God the second place, his wife is an idol, and God cannot hear his prayers.

Many a woman makes an idol of her children. Not that we can love our children too much. The more dearly we love Christ, the more dearly we love our children; but we can put our children in the wrong place, we can put them before God, and their interests before God's interests. When we do this our children are our idols.

Many a man makes an idol of his reputation or his business. Reputation or business is put before God. God cannot hear the prayers of such a man.

One great question for us to decide, if we would have power in prayer is, Is God absolutely first? Is He before wife, before children, before reputation, before business, before our own lives? If not, prevailing prayer is impossible.

God often calls our attention to the fact that we have an idol, by not answering our prayers, and thus leading us to inquire as to why our prayers are not answered, and so we discover the idol, put it away, and God hears our prayers.

4. The fourth hindrance to prayer is found in Prov. 21:13, *"Whoso stoppeth his ears at the cry of the poor,* he also shall cry himself, but shall not be heard."

There is perhaps no greater hindrance to prayer than stinginess, the lack of liberality toward the poor and toward God's work. It is the one who gives generously to others who receives generously from God.

HINDRANCES TO PRAYER

"Give, and it shall be given unto you; good measure, pressed down, shaken together, running over, shall they give into your bosom. For with what measure ye mete it shall be measured to you again." (Luke 6:38, R. V.) The generous man is the mighty man of prayer. The stingy man is the powerless man of prayer.

One of the most wonderful statements about prevailing prayer (already referred to) 1 John 3:22, "Whatsoever we ask we receive of Him, because we keep His commandments, and do those things that are pleasing in His sight," is made in direct connection with generosity toward the needy. In the context we are told that it is when we love, not in word or in tongue, but in deed and in truth, when we open our hearts toward the brother in need, it is then and only then we have confidence toward God in prayer.

Many a man and woman who is seeking to find the secret of their powerlessness in prayer need not seek far; it is nothing more nor less than downright stinginess. George Muller, to whom reference has already been made, was a mighty man of prayer because he was a mighty giver. What he received from God never stuck to his fingers; he immediately passed it on to others. He was constantly receiving because he was constantly giving. When one thinks of the selfishness of the professing church today, how the orthodox churches of this land do not average $1.00 per year per member for foreign missions, it is no wonder that the church has so little power in prayer. If we would get from God, we must give to others. Perhaps the most wonderful promise in the Bible in regard to God's supplying our need is Phil. 4:19, "And my God shall fulfill every need of yours according to His riches in glory in Christ Jesus." (R. V.) This glorious promise was made to the Philippian church, and made in immediate connection with their generosity.

5. The fifth hindrance to prayer is found in Mark 11:25, "And when ye stand praying, *forgive*, if ye have ought against any; that your Father also which is in heaven may forgive you your trespasses."

An unforgiving spirit is one of the commonest hindrances to prayer. Prayer is answered on the basis that our sins are forgiven; but God cannot deal with us on the basis of forgiveness while we are harboring illwill against those who have wronged us. Anyone who is nursing a grudge against another has fast closed the ear of God against his own petition. How many there are crying to God for the conversion of husband, children, friends, and wondering why it is that their prayer is not answered, when the whole secret is some grudge that they have in their hearts against someone who has injured them, or who they fancy has injured them. Many and many a mother and father are allowing their children to go down to eternity unsaved, for the miserable gratification of hating somebody.

6. The sixth hindrance to prayer is found in 1 Peter 3:7, "Ye husbands, in like manner, dwell with your wives according to knowledge, giving honor unto the woman, as unto the weaker vessel as being also joint-heirs of the grace of life; to the end that your prayers be not hindered." (R. V.) Here we are plainly told that *a wrong relation between husband and wife is a hindrance to prayer.*

In many and many a case the prayers of husbands are hindered because of their failure of duty toward their wives. On the other hand, it is also doubtless true that the prayers of wives are hindered because of their failure in duty toward their husbands. If husbands and wives should seek diligently to find the cause of their unanswered prayers, they would often find it in their relations to one another.

Many a man who makes great pretentions to piety, and is very active in Christian work, shows but little consideration in his treatment of his wife, and is oftentimes unkind, if not brutal; then he wonders why it is that his prayers are not answered. The verse that we have just quoted explains the seeming mystery. On the other hand, many a woman who is very devoted to the church, and very faithful in attendance upon all services, treats her husband with the most unpardonable neglect, is cross and peevish toward him, wounds him by the sharpness of her speech, and by her ungovernable temper; then wonders why it is that she has no power in prayer.

There are other things in the relations of husbands and wives which cannot be spoken of publicly, but which doubtless are oftentimes a hindrance in approaching God in prayer. There is much sin covered up under the holy name of marriage that is a cause of spiritual deadness, and of powerlessness in prayer. Any man or woman whose prayers seem to bring no answer should spread their whole married life out before God, and ask Him to put His finger upon anything in it that is displeasing in His sight.

7. The seventh hindrance to prayer is found in James 1:5–7, "But if any of you lacketh wisdom, let him ask of God, who giveth to all liberally

HINDRANCES TO PRAYER

and upbraideth not; and it shall be given him. But let him ask *in faith, nothing doubting*: for he that doubteth is like the surge of the sea driven by the wind and tossed. For let not that man think that he shall receive anything of the Lord." (R. V.)

Prayers are hindered by unbelief. God demands that we shall believe His Word absolutely. To question it is to make Him a liar. Many of us do that when we plead His promises, and is it any wonder that our prayers are not answered? How many prayers are hindered by our wretched unbelief! We go to God and ask Him for something that is positively promised in His Word, and then we do not more than half expect to get it. "For let not that man think that he shall receive anything of the Lord."

Chapter X
WHEN TO PRAY

If we would know the fullness of blessing that there is in the prayer life, it is important not only that we pray in the right way, but also that we pray at the right time. Christ's own example is full of suggestiveness as to the right time for prayer.

1. In the 1st chapter of Mark, the 35th verse, we read, "And *in the morning,* rising up *a great while before day,* He went out, and departed into a solitary place, and there prayed."

Jesus chose the early morning hour for prayer. Many of the mightiest men of God have followed the Lord's example in this. In the morning hour the mind is fresh and at its very best. It is free from distraction, and that absolute concentration upon God which is essential to the most effective prayer is most easily possible in the early morning hours. Furthermore, when the early hours are spent in prayer, the whole day is sanctified, and power is obtained for overcoming its temptations, and for performing its duties. More can be accomplished in prayer in the first hours of the day than at any other time during the day. Every child of God who would make the most out of his life for Christ, should set apart the first part of the day to meeting God in the study of His Word and in prayer. The first thing we do each day should be to go alone with God and face the duties, the temptations, and the service of that day, and get strength from God for all. We should get victory before the hour of trial, temptation or service comes. The secret place of prayer is the place to fight our battles and gain our victories.

2. In the 6th chapter of Luke in the 12th verse, we get further light upon the right time to pray. We read, "And it came to pass in those days, that He went out into a mountain to pray, and continued *all night* in prayer to God."

Here we see Jesus praying in the night, spending the entire night in prayer. Of course we have no reason to suppose that this was the constant practice of our Lord, nor do we even know how common this practice was, but there were certainly times when the whole night was given up to prayer. Here too we do well to follow in the footsteps of the Master.

Of course there is a way of setting apart nights for prayer in which there is no profit; it is pure legalism. But the abuse of this practice is no reason for neglecting it altogether. One ought not to say, "I am going to spend a whole night in prayer," with the thought that there is any merit that will win God's favor in such an exercise; that is legalism. But we oftentimes do well to say, "I am going to set apart this night for meeting God, and obtaining His blessing and power; and if necessary, and if He so leads me, I will give the whole night to prayer." Oftentimes we will have prayed things through long before the night has passed, and we can retire and find more refreshing and invigorating sleep than if we had not spent the time in prayer. At other times God doubtless will keep us in communion with Himself way into the morning, and when He does this in His infinite grace, blessed indeed are these hours of night prayer!

Nights of prayer to God are followed by days of power with men. In the night hours the world is hushed in slumber, and we can easily be alone with God and have undisturbed communion with Him. If we set apart the whole night for prayer, there will be no hurry, there will be time for our own hearts to become quiet before God, there will be time for the whole mind to be brought under the guidance of the Holy Spirit, there will be plenty of time to pray things through. A night of prayer should be put entirely under God's control. We should lay down no rules as to how long we will pray, or as to what we shall pray about, but be ready to wait upon God for a short time or a long time as He may lead, and to be led out in one direction or another as He may see fit.

3. Jesus Christ prayed *before all the great crises in His earthly life.*

He prayed before choosing the twelve disciples; before the sermon on the mount; before starting out on an evangelistic tour; before His anointing with the Holy Spirit and His entrance upon His public ministry; before announcing to the twelve His approaching death; before the great consummation of His life at the cross. (Luke 6:12, 13; Luke 9:18, 21, 22; Luke 3:21, 22; Mark 1:35–38; Luke 22:39–46.) He prepared for every important crisis by a protracted season of prayer. So ought we to do also. Whenever any crisis of life is seen to be approaching, we should prepare for it by a season of very definite prayer to God. We should take plenty of time for this prayer.

4. Christ prayed not only before the great events and victories of His life, but He also prayed *after its great achievements and important crises.*

When He had fed the five thousand with the five loaves and two fishes, and the multitude desired to take Him and make Him king, having sent them away He went up into the mountain apart to pray, and spent hours there alone in prayer to God (Matt. 14:23; Jno. 6:15). So He went on from victory to victory.

It is more common for most of us to pray before the great events of life than it is to pray after them, but the latter is as important as the former. If we would pray after the great achievements of life, we might go on to still greater; as it is we are often either puffed up or exhausted by the things that we do in the name of the Lord, and so we advance no further. Many and many a man in answer to prayer has been endued with power and thus has wrought great things in the name of the Lord, and when these great things were accomplished, instead of going alone with God and humbling himself before Him, and giving Him all the glory for what was achieved, he has congratulated himself upon what has been accomplished, has become puffed up, and God has been obliged to lay him aside. The great things done were not followed by humiliation of self, and prayer to God, and so pride has come in and the mighty man has been shorn of his power.

5. Jesus Christ gave a special time to prayer *when life was unusually busy.* He would withdraw at such a time from the multitudes that thronged about Him, and go into the wilderness and pray. For example, we read in Luke 5:15, 16, "But so much the more went abroad the report concerning Him: and great multitudes came together to hear, and to be healed of their infirmities. But He withdrew Himself in the deserts and prayed." (R. V.)

Some men are so busy that they find no time for prayer. Apparently the busier Christ's life was, the more He prayed. Sometimes He had no time to eat (Mark 3:20), sometimes He had no time for needed rest and sleep (Mark 6:31, 33, 46), but He always took time to pray; and the more the work crowded the more He prayed.

Many a mighty man of God has learned this secret from Christ, and when the work has crowded more than usual they have set an unusual amount of time apart for prayer. Other men of God, Once mighty, have lost their power because they did not learn this secret, and allowed increasing work to crowd out prayer.

Years ago it was the writer's privilege, with other theological students, to ask questions of one of the most useful Christian men of the day. The writer was led to ask,

"Will you tell us something of your prayer life?"

The man was silent a moment, and then, turning his eyes earnestly upon me, replied:

"Well, I must admit that I have been so crowded with work of late that I have not given the time I should to prayer."

Is it any wonder that that man lost power, and the great work that he was doing was curtailed in a very marked degree? Let us never forget that the more the work presses on us, the more time must we spend in prayer.

6. Jesus Christ prayed *before the great temptations of His life.*

As He drew nearer and nearer to the cross, and realized that upon it was to come the great final test of His life, Jesus went out into the garden to pray. He came "unto a place called Gethsemane, and saith unto the disciples, Sit ye here while I go and pray yonder." (Matt. 26:36.) The victory of Calvary was won that night in the garden of Gethsemane. The calm majesty of His bearing in meeting the awful onslaughts of Pilate's Judgment Hall and of Calvary, was the outcome of the struggle, agony and victory of Gethsemane. While Jesus prayed the disciples slept, so He stood fast while they fell ignominiously.

Many temptations come upon us unawares and unannounced, and all that we can do is to lift a cry to God for help then and there; but many of the temptations of life we can see approaching from the distance, and in such cases the victory should be won before the temptation really reaches us.

7. In 1 Thess. 5:17 we read, "Pray *without ceasing,*" and in Eph. 6:18, R. V., "praying *at all seasons.*"

Our whole life should be a life of prayer. We should walk in constant communion with God. There should be a constant upward looking of the soul to God. We should walk so habitually in His presence that even when we awake in the night it would be the most natural thing in the world for us to speak to Him in thanksgiving or in petition.

CHAPTER XI
THE NEED OF A GENERAL REVIVAL

If we are to pray aright in such a time as this, much of our prayer should be for a general revival. If there was ever a time in which there was need to cry unto God in the words of the Psalmist, "Wilt Thou not revive us again, that Thy people may rejoice in Thee?" (Ps. 85:6), it is this day in which we live. It is surely time for the Lord to work, for men have made void His law (Ps. 119:126). The voice of the Lord given in the written Word is set at naught both by the world and the church. Such a time is not a time for discouragement — the man who believes in God and believes in the Bible can never be discouraged; but it is a time for Jehovah Himself to step in and work. The intelligent Christian, the wide-awake watchman on the walls of Zion, may well cry with the Psalmist of old, "It is time for Thee Lord to work, for they have made void Thy law." (Ps. 119:126, Am. R. V.)

The great need of the day is a general revival.

Let us consider first of all what a general revival is.

A revival is a time of quickening or impartation of life. As God alone can give life, a revival is a time when God visits His people and by the power of His Spirit imparts new life to them, and through them imparts life to sinners dead in trespasses and sins. We have religious excitements gotten up by the cunning methods and hypnotic influence of the mere professional evangelist; but these are not revivals and are not needed. They are the devil's imitations of a revival. *New life from God* — that is a revival. A general revival is a time when this new life from God is not confined to scattered localities, but is general throughout Christendom and the earth.

The reason why a general revival is needed is that spiritual dearth and desolation and death is general. It is not confined to any one country, though it may be more manifest in some countries than in others. It is found in foreign mission fields as well as in home fields. We have had local revivals. The life-giving Spirit of God has breathed upon this minister and that, this church and that, this community and that; but we need, we sorely need, a revival that shall be widespread and general.

Let us look for a few moments at the results of a revival. These results are apparent in ministers, in the church and in the unsaved.

1. The results of a revival in a minister are:

(1) The minister has a new love for souls. We ministers as a rule have no such love for souls as we ought to have, no such love for souls as Jesus had, no such love for souls as Paul had. But when God visits His people the hearts of ministers are greatly burdened for the unsaved. They go out in great longing for the salvation of their fellowmen. They forget their ambition to preach great sermons and for fame, and simply long to see men brought to Christ.

(2) When true revivals come, ministers get a new love for God's Word and a new faith in God's Word. They fling to the winds their doubts and criticisms of the Bible and of the creeds, and go to preaching the Bible and especially Christ crucified. Revivals make ministers who are loose in their doctrines orthodox. A genuine wide-sweeping revival would do more to turn things upside down and thus get them right side up than all the heresy trials ever instituted.

(3) Revivals bring to ministers new liberty and power in preaching. It is no week-long grind to prepare a sermon, and no nerve-consuming effort to preach it after it has been prepared. Preaching is a joy and a refreshment, and there is power in it in times of revival.

2. The results of a revival on Christians generally are as marked as its results upon the ministry.

(1) In times of revival Christians come out from the world and live separated lives. Christians who have been dallying with the world, who have been playing cards and dancing and going to the theater and indulging in similar follies, give them up. These things are found to be incompatible with increasing life and light.

(2) In times of revival Christians get a new spirit of prayer. Prayer meetings are no longer a duty, but become the necessity of a hungry, importunate heart. Private prayer is followed with new zest. The voice of earnest prayer to God is heard day and night. People no longer ask, "Does God answer prayer?" They know He does, and besiege the throne of grace day and night.

(3) In times of revival Christians go to work for lost souls. They do not go to meeting simply to enjoy themselves and get blessed. They go

to meeting to watch for souls and to bring them to Christ. They talk to men on the street and in the stores and in their homes. The cross of Christ, salvation, heaven and hell become the subjects of constant conversation. Politics and the weather and new bonnets and the latest novels are forgotten.

(4) In times of revival Christians have new joy in Christ. Life is joy, and new life is new joy. Revival days are glad days, days of heaven on earth.

(5) In times of revival Christians get a new love for the Word of God. They want to study it day and night. Revivals are bad for saloons and theaters, but they are good for bookstores and Bible agencies.

3. But revivals also have a decided influence on the unsaved world.

(1) First of all, they bring deep conviction of sin. Jesus said that when the Spirit was come He would convince the world of sin (Jno. 16:7, 8). Now we have seen that a revival is coming of the Holy Spirit, and therefore there must be new conviction of sin, and there always is. If you see something men call a revival, and there is no conviction of sin, you may know at once that it is bogus. It is a sure mark.

(2) Revivals bring also conversion and regeneration. When God refreshes His people, He always converts sinners also. The first result of Pentecost was new life and power to the one hundred and twenty disciples in the upper room; the second result was three thousand conversions in a single day. It is always so. I am constantly reading of revivals here and there, where Christians were greatly helped but there were no conversions. I have my doubts about that kind. If Christians are truly refreshed, they will get after the unsaved by prayer and testimony and persuasion, and there will be conversions.

WHY A GENERAL REVIVAL IS NEEDED

We see what a general revival is, and what it does; let us now face the question why it is needed at the present time.

I think that the mere description of what it is and what it does shows that it is needed, sorely needed, but let us look at some specific conditions that exist today that show the need of it. In showing these conditions one is likely to be called a pessimist. If facing the facts is to be called a pessimist, I am willing to be called a pessimist. If in order to be an optimist one must shut his eyes and call black white, and error truth,

THE NEED OF A GENERAL REVIVAL

and sin righteousness, and death life, I don't want to be called an optimist. But I am an optimist all the same. Pointing out the real condition will lead to a better condition.

1. Look first at the ministry.

(1) Many of us who are professedly orthodox ministers are practically infidels. That is plain speech, but it is also indisputable fact. There is no essential difference between the teachings of Tom Paine and Bob Ingersoll and the teachings of some of our theological professors. The latter are not so blunt and honest about it; they phrase it in more elegant and studied sentences; but it means the same. Much of the so-called new learning and higher criticism is simply Tom Paine infidelity sugar coated. Prof. Howard Osgood, who was a real scholar and not a mere echo of German infidelity, once read a statement of some positions, and asked if they did not fairly represent the scholarly criticism of today, and when it was agreed that they did, he startled his audience by saying:

"I am reading from Tom Paine's 'Age of Reason.' "

There is little new in the higher criticism. Our future ministers oftentimes are being educated under infidel professors, and being immature boys when they enter the college or seminary, they naturally come out infidels in many cases, and then go forth to poison the church.

(2) Even when our ministers are orthodox — as thank God so very many are! — they are oftentimes not men of prayer. How many modern ministers know what it is to wrestle in prayer, to spend a good share of a night in prayer? I do not know how many, but I do know that many do not.

(3) Many of us who are ministers have no love for souls. How many preach because they *must* preach, because they feel that men everywhere are perishing, and by preaching they hope to save some? And how many follow up their preaching as Paul did, by beseeching men everywhere to be reconciled to God?

Perhaps enough has been said about us ministers; but it is evident that a revival is needed for our sake, or some of us will have to stand before God overwhelmed with confusion in an awful day of reckoning that is surely coming.

2. Look now at the church:

(1) Look at the doctrinal state of the church. It is bad enough. Many do not believe in the whole Bible. The book of Genesis is a myth, Jonah

is an allegory, and even the miracles of the Son of God are questioned. The doctrine of prayer is old-fashioned, and the work of the Holy Spirit is sneered at. Conversion is unnecessary, and hell is no longer believed in.

(2) Look at the spiritual state of the church. Worldliness is rampant among church members. Many church members are just as eager as any in the rush to get rich. They use the methods of the world in the accumulation of wealth, and they hold just as fast to it as any when they have gotten it.

Prayerlessness abounds among church members on every hand. Someone has said that Christians on the average do not spend more than five minutes a day in prayer.

Neglect of the Word of God goes hand in hand with neglect of prayer to God. Very many Christians spend twice as much time every day wallowing through the mire of the daily papers as they do bathing in the cleansing laver of God's Holy Word. How many Christians average an hour a day spent in Bible study?

Along with neglect of prayer and neglect of the Word of God goes a lack of generosity. The churches are rapidly increasing in wealth, but the treasuries of the missionary societies are empty. Christians do not average a dollar a year for foreign missions. It is simply appalling.

Then there is the increasing disregard for the Lord's Day. It is fast becoming a day of worldly pleasure, instead of a day of holy service. The Sunday newspaper with its inane twaddle and filthy scandal takes the place of the Bible; and visiting and golf and bicycle, the place of the Sunday school and church service.

Christians mingle with the world in all forms of questionable amusements. The young man or young woman who does not believe in dancing with its rank immodesties, the card table with its drift toward gambling, and the theater with its ever-increasing appeal to lewdness, is counted an old fogy.

Then how small a proportion of our membership has really entered into fellowship with Jesus Christ in His burden for souls! Enough has been said of the spiritual state of the church.

3. Now look at the state of the world.

(1) Not how few conversions there are. Here and there a church has a large number of accessions upon confession of faith, but these churches are rare exceptions; and where there are such accessions, in

how few cases are the conversions deep, thorough and satisfactory.

(2) There is lack of conviction of sin. Seldom are men overwhelmed with a sense of their awful guilt in trampling under foot the Son of God. Sin is regarded as a "misfortune" or as "infirmity," or even as "good in the making"; seldom as enormous wrong against a holy God.

(3) Unbelief is rampant. Many regard it as a mark of intellectual superiority to reject the Bible, and even faith in God and immortality. It is about the only mark of intellectual superiority many possess, and perhaps that is the reason they cling to it so tenaciously.

(4) Hand in hand with this widespread infidelity goes gross immorality, as has always been the case. Infidelity and immorality are Siamese twins. They always exist and always grow and always fatten together. This prevailing immorality is found everywhere.

This immorality is found in the theater. The theater at its best is bad enough, but now the "Sapphos," and the "Degenerates," and all the unspeakable vile accessories of the stage rule the day, and the women who debauch themselves by appearing in such plays are defended in the newspapers and welcomed by supposedly respectable people.

Much of our literature is rotten. Art is oftentimes a mere covering for shameless indecency. Women are induced to cast modesty to the winds that the artist may perfect his art and defile his morals.

Greed for money has become a mania with rich and poor. The multimillionaire will often sell his soul and trample the rights of his fellowmen underfoot in the mad hope of becoming a billionaire, and the laboring man will often commit murder to increase the power of the union and keep up wages. Wars are waged and men shot down like dogs to improve commerce, and to gain political prestige for unprincipled politicians who parade as statesmen.

The licentiousness of the day lifts its serpent head everywhere. You see it in the newspapers, you see it on the billboards, you see it on the advertisements of cigars, shoes, bicycles, patent medicines, corsets and everything else. You see it on the streets at night. You see it just outside the church door. You find it not only in the awful cesspools set apart for it in the great cities, but it is crowding further and further up our business streets and into the residence portions of our cities. Alas! now and then you find it, if you look sharp, in supposedly respectable homes; indeed it will be borne to your ears by the confessions of brokenhearted men and women. The moral condition of the world in our day is disgusting, sickening, appalling.

We need a revival, deep, widespread, general, in the power of the Holy Ghost. It is either a general revival or the dissolution of the church, of the home, of the state. A revival, new life from God, is the cure, and the only cure. That will stem the awful tide of immorality and unbelief. Mere argument will not do it; but a wind from heaven, a new outpouring of the Holy Ghost, a true God-sent revival will. I believe that breath from God is coming.

The great need of today is a general revival. The need is clear. It admits of no honest difference of opinion. What then shall we do? Pray. Take up the Psalmist's prayer, "Revive us again, that Thy people may rejoice in Thee." Take up Ezekiel's prayer, "Come from the four winds, O breath (breath of God), and breathe upon these slain that they may live." Hark, I hear a noise! Behold a shaking! I can almost feel the breeze upon my cheek. I can almost see the great living army rising to their feet. Shall we not pray and pray and pray and pray, till the Spirit comes, and God revives His people?

Chapter XII
THE PLACE OF PRAYER
BEFORE AND DURING REVIVALS

No treatment of the subject "How to Pray" would be at all complete if it did not consider the place of prayer in revivals.

The first great revival of Christian history had its origin on the human side in a ten days' prayer meeting. We read of that handful of disciples, "These all with one accord continued steadfastly in prayer." (Acts 1:14, R. V.) The result of that prayer meeting we read of in the 2d chapter of the Acts of the Apostles, "They were all filled with the Holy Ghost, and began to speak with other tongues, as the Spirit gave them utterance." (Verse 4.) Further on in the chapter we read that "there were added unto them in that day about three thousand souls." (Verse 41, R. V.) This revival proved genuine and permanent. The converts "continued steadfastly in the apostles' teaching and fellowship, in the breaking of bread and the prayers." (Verse 42, R. V.) "And the Lord added to them day by day those that were being saved." (Verse 47, R. V.)

Every true revival from that day to this has had its earthly origin in prayer. The great revival under Jonathan Edwards in the eighteenth century began with his famous call to prayer. The marvelous work of grace among the Indians under Brainerd had its origin in the days and nights that Brainerd spent before God in prayer for an enduement of power from on high for this work.

A most remarkable and widespread display of God's reviving power was that which broke out at Rochester, New York, in 1830, under the labors of Charles G. Finney. It not only spread throughout the state but ultimately to Great Britian as well. Mr. Finney himself attributed the power of this work to the spirit of prayer that prevailed. He describes it in his autobiography in the following words:

"When I was on my way to Rochester, as we passed through a village, some thirty miles east of Rochester, a brother minister whom I knew, seeing me on the canal boat, jumped aboard to have a little conversation with me, intending to ride but a little way and return. He, however, became interested in conversation, and upon finding where I was going, he made up his mind to keep on and go with me to Rochester. We had been there but a few days when this minister became so convicted that he could not help weeping aloud at one time as we passed along the street. The Lord gave him a powerful spirit of prayer, and his heart was broken. As he and I prayed together, I was struck with his faith in regard to what the Lord was going to do there. I recollect he would say, 'Lord, I do not know how it is; but I seem to know that Thou art going to do a great work in this city.' The spirit of prayer was poured out powerfully, so much so that some persons stayed away from the public services to pray, being unable to restrain their feelings under preaching.

"And here I must introduce the name of a man, whom I shall have occasion to mention frequently, Mr. Abel Clary. He was the son of a very excellent man, and an elder of the church where I was converted. He was converted in the same revival in which I was. He had been licensed to preach; but his spirit of prayer was such, he was so burdened with the souls of men, that he was not able to preach much, his whole time and strength being given to prayer. The burden of his soul would frequently be so great that he was unable to stand, and he would writhe and groan in agony. I was well acquainted with him, and knew something of the wonderful spirit of prayer that was upon him. He was a very silent man, as almost all are who have that powerful spirit of prayer.

"The first I knew of his being in Rochester, a gentleman who lived about a mile west of the city, called on me one day and asked me if I knew a Mr. Abel Clary, a minister. I told him that I knew him well. 'Well,' he said, 'he is at my house, and has been there for some time, and I don't know what to think of him.' I said, 'I have not seen him at any of our meetings.' 'No,' he replied, 'he cannot go to meeting, he says. He prays nearly all the time, day and night, and in such agony of mind that I do not know what to make of it. Sometimes he cannot even stand on his knees, but will lie prostrate on the floor, and groan and pray in a manner that quite astonishes me.' I said to the brother, 'I understand it: please keep still. It will all come out right; he will surely prevail.'

"I knew at the time a considerable number of men who were exercised in the same way. A Deacon P____, of Camden, Oneida county;

THE PLACE OF PRAYER 57

a Deacon T____, of Rodman, Jefferson county; a Deacon B____, of Adams, in the same county; this Mr. Clary and many others among the men, and a large number of women partook of the same spirit, and spent a great part of their time in prayer. Father Nash, as we called him, who in several of my fields of labor came to me and aided me, was another of those men that had such a powerful spirit of prevailing prayer. This Mr. Clary continued in Rochester as long as I did, and did not leave it until after I had left. He never, that I could learn, appeared in public, but gave himself wholly to prayer.

"I think it was the second Sabbath that I was at Auburn at this time, I observed in the congregation the solemn face of Mr. Clary. He looked as if he was borne down with an agony of prayer. Being well acquainted with him, and knowing the great gift of God that was upon him, the spirit of prayer, I was very glad to see him there. He sat in the pew with his brother, the doctor, who was also a professor of religion, but who had nothing by experience, I should think, of his brother Abel's great power with God.

"At intermission, as soon as I came down from the pulpit, Mr. Clary, with his brother, met me at the pulpit stairs, and the doctor invited me to go home with him and spend the intermission and get some refreshments. I did so.

"After arriving at his house we were soon summoned to the dinner table. We gathered about the table, and Dr. Clary turned to his brother and said, 'Brother Abel, will you ask the blessing?' Brother Abel bowed his head and began, audibly, to ask a blessing. He had uttered but a sentence or two when he broke instantly down, moved suddenly back from the table, and fled to his chamber. The doctor supposed he had been taken suddenly ill, and rose up and followed him. In a few moments he came down and said, 'Mr. Finney, brother Abel wants to see you.' Said I, 'What ails him?' Said he, 'I do not know but he says; you know. He appears in great distress, but I think it is the state of his mind.' I understood it in a moment, and went to his room. He lay groaning upon the bed, the Spirit making intercession for him, and in him, with groanings that could not be uttered. I had barely entered the room, when he made out to say, 'Pray, brother Finney.' I knelt down and helped him in prayer, by leading his soul out for the conversion of sinners. I continued to pray until his distress passed away, and then I returned to the dinner table.

"I understood that this was the voice of God. I saw the spirit of prayer was upon him, and I felt his influence upon myself, and took it for granted that the work would move on powerfully. It did so. The pastor told me afterward that he found that in the six weeks that I was there, five hundred souls had been converted."

Mr. Finney in his lectures on revivals tells of other remarkable awakenings in answer to the prayers of God's people. He says in one place, "A clergyman in W____n told me of a revival among his people, which commenced with a zealous and devoted woman in the church. She became anxious about sinners, and went to praying for them; she prayed, and her distress increased; and she finally came to her minister, and talked with him, and asked him to appoint an anxious meeting, for she felt that one was needed. The minister put her off, for he felt nothing of it. The next week she came again, and besought him to appoint an anxious meeting; she knew there would be somebody to come, for she felt as if God was going to pour out His Spirit. He put her off again. And finally she said to him, 'If you do not appoint an anxious meeting I shall die, for there is certainly going to be a revival.' The next Sabbath he appointed a meeting, and said that if there were any who wished to converse with him about the salvation of their souls, he would meet them on such an evening. He did not know of one, but when he went to the place, to his astonishment he found a large number of anxious inquirers."

In still another place he says, "The first ray of light that broke in upon the midnight which rested on the churches in Oneida county, in the fall of 1825, was from a woman in feeble health, who, I believe, had never been in a powerful revival. Her soul was exercised about sinners. She was in agony for the land. She did not know what ailed her, but she kept praying more and more, till it seemed as if her agony would destroy her body. At length she became full of joy and exclaimed, 'God has come! God has come! There is no mistake about it, the work is begun, and is going over all the region!' And sure enough, the work began, and her family were almost all converted, and the work spread all over that part of the country."

The great revival of 1857 in the United States began in prayer and was carried on by prayer more than by anything else. Dr. Cuyler in an article in a religious newspaper some years ago said, "Most revivals have humble beginnings, and the fire starts in a few warm hearts. Never despise the day of small things. During all my own long ministry, nearly every work of grace had a similar beginning. One commenced in a meeting gathered at a few hours' notice in a private house. Another commenced in a group gathered for Bible study by Mr. Moody in our mission chapel. Still another — the most powerful of all — was kindled on a bitter January evening at a meeting of young Christians under my roof. Dr. Spencer, in his 'Pastor's Sketches' (the most suggestive book of its kind I have ever read), tells us that a remarkable revival in his church sprang from the fervent prayers of a godly old man who was confined to his room by lameness. That profound Christian, Dr. Thomas H. Skinner, of the Union Theological Seminary, once gave me an account of a remarkable coming together of three earnest men in his study when he was the pastor of the Arch Street Church in Philadelphia. They literally wrestled in prayer. They made a clean breast in confession of sin, and humbled themselves before God. One and another church officer came in and joined them. The heaven-kindled flame soon spread through the whole congregation in one of the most powerful revivals ever known in that city."

In the early part of the sixteenth century there was a great religious awakening in Ulster, Ireland. The lands of the rebel chiefs which had been forfeited to the British crown, were settled up by a class of colonists who for the most part were governed by a spirit of wild adventure. Real piety was rare. Seven ministers, five from Scotland and two from England, settled in that country, the earliest arrivals being in 1613. Of one of these ministers named Blair it is recorded by a contemporary, "He spent many days and nights in prayer, alone and with others, and was vouchsafed great intimacy with God." Mr. James Glendenning, a man of very meager natural gifts, was a man similarly minded as regards prayer. The work began under this man Glendenning. The historian of the time says, "He was a man who never would have been chosen by a wise assembly of ministers, nor sent to begin a reformation in this land. Yet this was the Lord's choice to begin with him the admirable work of God which I mention on purpose that all may see how the glory is only the Lord's in making a holy nation in this profane land, and that it was 'not by might, nor by power, nor by man's wisdom, but by My Spirit, saith the Lord.' " In his preaching at Oldstone multitudes of hearers felt in great anxiety and terror of conscience. They looked on themselves as altogether lost and damned, and cried out, "Men and brethren, what shall we do to be saved?" They were stricken into a swoon by the power of His Word. A dozen in one day were carried out-of-doors as dead. These were not women, but some of the boldest spirits of the neighborhood; "some who had formerly feared not with their swords to put a whole market town into a fray." Concerning one of them, the historian writes, "I have heard one of them, then a mighty strong man, now a mighty Christian, say that his end in coming into church was to consult with his companions how to work some mischief."

This work spread throughout the whole country. By the year 1626 a monthly concert of prayer was held in Antrim. The work spread beyond the bounds of Down and Antrim to the churches of the neighboring counties. So great became the religious interest that Christians would come thirty or forty miles to the communions, and continue from the time they came until they returned without wearying or making use of sleep. Many of them neither ate nor drank, and yet some of them professed that they "went away most fresh and vigorous, their souls so filled with the sense of God."

This revival changed the whole character of northern Ireland.

Another great awakening in Ireland in 1859 had a somewhat similar origin. By many who did not know, it was thought that this marvelous work came without warning and preparation, but Rev. William Gibson, the moderator of the General Assembly of the Presbyterian Church in Ireland in 1860, in his very interesting and valuable history of the work tells how there had been preparation for two years. There had been constant discussion in the General Assembly of the low estate of religion, and of the need of a revival. There had been special sessions for prayer. Finally four young men, who became leaders in the origin of the great work, began to meet together in an old schoolhouse in the neighborhood of Kells. About the spring of 1858 a work of power began to manifest itself. It spread from town to town, and from county to county. The congregations became too large for the buildings, and the meetings were held in the open air, oftentimes attended by many thousands of people. Many hundreds of persons were frequently convicted of sin in a single meeting. In some places the criminal courts and jails were closed for lack of occupation. There were manifestations of the Holy Spirit's power of a most remarkable character, clearly proving that the Holy Spirit is as ready to work today as in apostolic days, when

THE PLACE OF PRAYER

ministers and Christians really believe in Him and begin to prepare the way by prayer.

Mr. Moody's wonderful work in England and Scotland and Ireland that afterwards spread to America had its origin on the manward side in prayer. Mr. Moody made little impression until men and women began to cry to God. Indeed his going to England at all was in answer to the importunate cries to God of a bedridden saint. While the spirit of prayer continued the revival abode in strength, but in the course of time less and less was made of prayer and the work fell off very perceptibly in power. Doubtless one of the great secrets of the unsatisfactoriness and superficiality and unreality of many of our modern so-called revivals, is that more dependence is put upon man's machinery than upon God's power, sought and obtained by earnest, persistent, believing prayer. We live in a day characterized by the multiplication of man's machinery and the diminution of God's power. The great cry of our day is work, work, work, new organizations, new methods, new machinery; the great need of our day is prayer. It was a master stroke of the devil when he got the church so generally to lay aside this mighty weapon of prayer. The devil is perfectly willing that the church should multiply its organizations, and deftly contrive machinery for the conquest of the world for Christ if it will only give up praying. He laughs as he looks at the church today and says to himself:

"You can have your Sunday schools and your young people's groups, your Institutional Churches and your church suppers, your grand choirs and your fine organs, your brilliant preachers and your revival efforts too, if you don't bring the power of Almighty God into them by earnest, persistent, believing, mighty prayer."

Prayer could work as marvelous results today as it ever could, if the church would only betake itself to it.

There seems to be increasing signs that the church is awaking to this fact. Here and there God is laying upon individual ministers and churches a burden of prayer that they have never known before. Less dependence is being put upon machinery and more dependence upon God. Ministers are crying to God day and night for power. Churches and portions of churches are meeting together in the early morning hours and the late night hours crying to God for the latter rain. There is every indication of the coming of a mighty and widespread revival. There is every reason why, if a revival should come in any country at this time, it should be more widespread in its extent than any revival of history. There is the closest and swiftest communication by travel, by letter, and by cable between all parts of the world. A true fire of God kindled in America would soon spread to the uttermost parts of the earth. The only thing needed to bring this fire is prayer.

It is not necessary that the whole church get to praying to begin with. Great revivals always begin first in the hearts of a few men and women whom God arouses by His Spirit to believe in Him as a living God, as a God who answers prayer, and upon whose heart He lays a burden from which no rest can be found except in importunate crying unto God.

May God use this book to arouse many others to pray that the greatly needed revival may come, and come speedily.

LET US PRAY

ANSWERS TO PRAYER

by

George Müller

CONTENTS

CHAPTER	PAGE
How To Ascertain the Will of God	ii
1 Beginning and Early Days of the Orphan Work	1
2 The New Orphan Houses, Ashley Down	22
3 Precious Answers to Prayer	31
Appendix A	68
Appendix B	69
Appendix C	73

HOW TO ASCERTAIN THE WILL OF GOD

I SEEK at the beginning to get my heart into such a state that it has no will of its own in regard to a given matter. Nine-tenths of the trouble with people generally is just here. Nine-tenths of the difficulties are overcome when our hearts are ready to do the Lord's will, whatever it may be. When one is truly in this state, it is usually but a little way to the knowledge of what His will is.

2.—Having done this, I do not leave the result to feeling or simple impression. If so, I make myself liable to great delusions.

3.—I seek the Will of the Spirit of God through, or in connection with, the Word of God. The Spirit and the Word must be combined. If I look to the Spirit alone without the Word, I lay myself open to great delusions also. If the Holy Ghost guides us at all, He will do it according to the Scriptures and never contrary to them.

4.—Next I take into account providential circumstances. These often plainly indicate God's Will in connection with His Word and Spirit.

5.—I ask God in prayer to reveal His Will to me aright.

6.—Thus, through prayer to God, the study of the Word, and reflection, I come to a deliberate judgment according to the best of my ability and knowledge, and if my mind is thus at peace, and continues so after two or three more petitions, I proceed accordingly. In trivial matters, and in transactions involving most important issues, I have found this method always effective.

ANSWERS TO PRAYER

Chapter I
BEGINNING AND EARLY DAYS OF THE ORPHAN WORK

That the trial of your faith, being much more precious than of gold that perisheth, though it be tried with fire, might be found unto praise and honour and glory at the appearing of Jesus Christ.—I *Peter*, 1:7.

Mr. George Müeller, the founder of the New Orphan-Houses, Ashley Down, Bristol (institutions that have been for many years the greatest monuments of modern times to a prayer-answering God), gives in that most valuable and instructive book, "A Narrative of Some of the Lord's Dealings with George Müeller," Vol. I., among other reasons for establishing an Orphan-House, the following: —

"Sometimes I found children of God tried in mind by the prospect of old age, when they might be unable to work any longer, and therefore were harassed by the fear of having to go into the poorhouse. If in such a case I pointed out to them, how their Heavenly Father has always helped those who put their trust in Him, they might not, perhaps, always say, that times have changed; but yet it was evident enough, that God was not looked upon by them as the LIVING God. My spirit was ofttimes bowed down by this, and I longed to set something before the children of God, whereby they might see, that He does not forsake, even in our day, those who rely upon Him.

"Another class of persons were brethren in business, who suffered in their souls, and brought guilt on their consciences, by carrying on their business, almost in the same way as unconverted persons do. The competition in trade, the bad times, the overpeopled country, were given as reasons why, if the business were carried on simply according to the Word of God, it could not be expected to do well.

Such a brother, perhaps, would express the wish, that he might be differently situated; but very rarely did I see *that there was a stand made for God, that there was the holy determination to trust in the living God, and to depend on Him, in order that a good conscience might be maintained.* To this class likewise I desired to show, by a visible proof, that God is unchangeably the same.

"Then there was another class of persons, individuals who were in professions in which they could not continue with a good conscience, or persons who were in an unscriptural position with reference to spiritual things; but both classes feared, on account of the consequences, to give up the profession in which they could not abide with God, or to leave their position, lest they should be thrown out of employment. My spirit longed to be instrumental in strengthening their faith, by giving them not only instances from the word of God, of His willingness and ability to help all those who rely upon Him, but *to show them by proofs,* that He is the same in our day. I well knew *that the Word of God ought to be enough,* and it was, by grace, enough to me; but still, I considered that I ought to lend a helping hand to my brethren, if by any means, by this visible proof to the unchangeable faithfulness of the Lord, I might strengthen their hands in God; for I remembered what a great blessing my own soul had received through the Lord's dealings with His servant A. H. Franke, who in dependence upon the living God alone, established an immense Orphan-House, which I had seen many times with my own eyes. I, therefore, judged myself bound to be the servant of the Church of God, in the particular point on which I had obtained mercy: namely, *in being able to take God by His word and to rely upon it.* All these exercises of my soul, which resulted from the fact that so many believers, with whom I became acquainted, were harassed and distressed in mind, or brought guilt on their consciences, on account of not trusting in the Lord; were used by God to awaken in my heart the desire of setting before the church at large, and before the world, a proof that He was not in the least changed; and this seemed to me best done, by the establishing of an Orphan-House. It needed to be something which could be seen, even by the natural eye. Now, if I, a poor man, simply by prayer and faith, obtained *without asking any individual,* the means for establishing and carrying on an Orphan-House, there would be something which, with the Lord's blessing, might be instrumental in strengthening the faith of the children of God, besides

BEGINNING AND EARLY DAYS OF THE ORPHAN WORK

being a testimony to the consciences of the unconverted, of the reality of the things of God. This, then, was the primary reason for establishing the Orphan-House. I certainly did from my heart desire to be used by God to benefit the bodies of poor children, bereaved of both parents, and seek in other respects, with the help of God, to do them good for this life; — I also particularly longed to be used by God in getting the dear orphans trained up in the fear of God; — but still, the first and primary object of the work was (and still is:) that God might be magnified by the fact, that the orphans under my care are provided with all they need, only by *prayer and faith* without anyone being asked by me or my fellow-labourers whereby it may be seen, that God is FAITHFUL STILL, and HEARS PRAYER STILL. That I was not mistaken, has been abundantly proved since November, 1835, both by the conversion of many sinners who have read the accounts, which have been published in connection with this work, and also by the abundance of fruit that has followed in the hearts of the saints, for which from my inmost soul, I desire to be grateful to God, and the honor and glory of which not only is due to Him alone, but, which I, by His help, am enabled to ascribe to Him."

"OPEN THY MOUTH WIDE"

In the account written by Mr. Müeller dated Jan. 16, 1836, respecting the Orphan-House intended to be established in Bristol in connection with the Scriptural Knowledge Institution for Home and Abroad, we read: —

"When, of late, the thoughts of establishing an Orphan-House, in dependence upon the Lord, revived in my mind, during the first two weeks I only prayed that if it were of the Lord, he would bring it about, but if not that He graciously would be pleased to take all thoughts about it out of my mind. My uncertainty about knowing the Lord's mind did not arise from questioning whether it would be pleasing in His sight, that there should be an abode and Scriptural education provided for destitute fatherless and motherless children; but whether it were His will that I should be the instrument of setting such an object on foot, as my hands were already more than filled. My comfort, however, was, that, if it were His will, He would provide not merely the means, but also suitable individuals to take care of the children, so that my part of the work would take only such a portion of my time, as, considering the importance of the matter, I might give, notwithstanding my many other engagements. The whole of those two weeks I never asked the Lord for money or for persons to engage in the work.

"On December 5th, however, the subject of my prayer all at once became different. I was reading Psalm 81., and was particularly struck, more than at any time before, with verse 10: *"Open thy mouth wide, and I will fill it."* I thought a few moments about these words, and then was led to apply them to the case of the Orphan-House. It struck me that I had never asked the Lord for anything concerning it, except to know His will, respecting its being established or not; and I then fell on my knees and opened my mouth wide, asking Him for much. I asked in submission to His will, and without fixing a time when He should answer my petition. I prayed that He would give me a house, *i.e.*, either as a loan, or that someone might be led to pay the rent for one, or that one might be given permanently for this object; further, I asked Him for £1000; and likewise for suitable individuals to take care of the children. Besides this, I have been since led to ask the Lord, to put into the hearts of His people to send me articles of furniture for the house, and some clothes for the children. When I was asking the petition, I was fully aware what I was doing, *i.e.*, that I was asking for something which I had no natural prospect of obtaining from the brethren whom I know, but which was not too much for the Lord to grant."

"December 10, 1835. — This morning I received a letter, in which a brother and sister wrote thus: — 'We propose ourselves for the service of the intended Orphan-House, if you think us qualified for it; also to give up all the furniture, &C.' which the Lord has given us, for its use; and to this without receiving any salary whatever; believing that if it be the will of the Lord to employ us, He will supply all our needs, &C."

"Dec. 13. — A brother was influenced this day to give 4s. per week, or £10 8s. yearly, as long as the Lord gives the means; 8s. was given by him as two weeks' subscriptions. To-day a brother and sister offered themselves, with all their furniture, and all the provisions which they have in the house, if they can be usefully employed in the concerns of the Orphan-House."

A GREAT ENCOURAGEMENT

"Dec. 17. — I was rather cast down last evening and this morning about the matter, questioning whether I ought to be engaged in this way, and was led to ask the Lord to give me some further encouragement. Soon after were sent by a brother two pieces of print, the one seven and the other 23¾ yards, 6¾ yards of calico, four pieces of lining, about four yards altogether, a sheet, and a yard measure. This evening another brother brought a clothes horse, three frocks, four pinafores, six handkerchiefs, three counterpanes, one blanket, two pewter salt cellars, six tin cups, and six metal tea spoons; he also brought 3s 6d. given to him by three different individuals. At the same time he told me that it had been put into the heart of an individual to send tomorrow £100."

ONE THOUSAND POUNDS

"June 15, 1837. — To-day I gave myself once more earnestly to prayer respecting the remainder of the £1000. This evening £5 was given, so that now the whole sum is made up. To the Glory of the Lord, whose I am, and whom I serve, I would state again, that every shilling of this money, and all the articles of clothing and furniture, which have been mentioned in the foregoing pages, have been given to me, *without one single individual having been asked by me for anything.*"

ORPHANS FOR THE BUILDING

In a third statement, containing the announcement of the opening of the Orphan-House, for destitute female children, and a proposal for the establishment of an Infant Orphan-House, which was sent to the press on May 18, 1836, Mr. Müeller wrote: —
"So far as I remember, I brought even the most minute circumstances concerning the Orphan-House before the Lord in my petitions, being conscious of my own weakness and ignorance. There was, however, one point I never had prayed about, namely that the Lord would send children; for I naturally took it for granted that there would be plenty of applications. The nearer, however, the day came which had been appointed for receiving applications, the more I had a secret consciousness, that the Lord might disappoint my natural expectations, and show me that I could not prosper in one single thing without Him. The appointed time came, and not even one application was made. I

had before this been repeatedly tried, whether I might not, after all, against the Lord's mind, have engaged in the work. This circumstance now led me to lie low before my God in prayer the whole of the evening, February 3, and to examine my heart once more as to all the motives concerning it; and being able, as formerly, to say, that His glory was my *chief aim, i.e.*, that it might be seen that it is not a vain thing to trust in the living God, — and that my *second aim* was the spiritual welfare of the orphan-children, — and the *third* their bodily welfare; and still continuing in prayer, I was at last brought to this state, that I could say *from my heart*, that I should rejoice in God being glorified in this matter, though it were *by bringing the whole to nothing*. But as still, after all, it seemed to me more tending to the glory of God, to establish and prosper the Orphan-House, I could then ask Him heartily, to send applications. I enjoyed now a peaceful state of heart concerning the subject, and was also more assured than ever that God would establish it. *The very next day*, February 4, the first application was made, and since then 42 more have been made."

"JUST FOR TO-DAY"

Later on, when there were nearly 100 persons to be maintained, and the funds were reduced to about £20, Mr. Müeller writes: —

"July 22 [1838]. — This evening I was walking in our little garden, meditating on Heb. 13:8, 'Jesus Christ the same yesterday, and to-day, and for ever.' Whilst meditating on His unchangeable love, power, wisdom, &C. — and turning all, as I went on, into prayer respecting myself; and whilst applying likewise His unchangeable love, and power and wisdom, &C., both to my present spiritual and temporal circumstances: — all at once the present need of the Orphan-House was brought to my mind. Immediately I was led to say to myself, Jesus in His love and power has hitherto supplied me with what I have needed for the Orphans, and in the same unchangeable love and power He will provide with what I may need for the future. A flow of joy came into my soul whilst realising thus the unchangeableness of our adorable Lord. About one minute after, a letter was brought me, enclosing a bill for £20. In it was written: "Will you apply the amount of the enclosed bill to the furtherance of the objects of your Scriptural Knowledge Society, or of your Orphan Establishment, or in the work and cause of our Master in any way that He Himself, on your application to Him, may point out to you. It is not a great sum, but it is a sufficient provision for the exigency of to-day; and it is for *to-day's* exigencies, that, ordinarily, the Lord provides. To-morrow, as it brings its demands, will find its supply, etc."

"[Of this £20 I took £10 for the Orphan fund, and £10 for the other objects, and was thus enabled to meet the expenses of about £34 which, in connection with the Orphan-Houses, came upon me within four days afterwards, and which I knew beforehand would come.]"

WAITING FOR HELP

"Nov. 21, 1838. — Never were we so reduced in funds as to-day. There was not a single half-penny in hand between the matrons of the three houses. Nevertheless there was a good dinner, and by managing so as to help one another with bread, etc., there was a prospect of getting over this day also; but for none of the houses had we the prospect of being able to take in bread. When I left the brethren and sisters at one o'clock, after prayer, I told them that we must wait for help, and see how the Lord would deliver us this time. I was sure of help, but we were indeed straitened. When I came to Kingsdown, I felt that I needed more exercise, being very old; wherefore I went on the nearest way home, but round by Clarence Place. About twenty yards from my house, I met a brother who walked back with me, and after a little conversation gave me £10 to be handed over to the brethren, the deacons, towards providing the poor saints with coal, blankets and warm clothing; also £5 for the Orphans, and £5 for the other objects of the Scriptural Knowledge Institution. The brother had called twice while I was gone to the Orphan-Houses, and had I now been *one half minute* later, I should have missed him. But the Lord knew our need, and therefore allowed me to meet him. I sent off the £5 immediately to the matrons."

BEYOND DISAPPOINTMENT

"Sept. 21 [1840], Monday. By what was in the hand of the Orphans, and by what had come in yesterday, the need of to-day is more than supplied, as there is enough for to-morrow also. To-day a brother from the neighbourhood of London gave me £10, to be laid out as it might be most needed. As we have been praying many days for the School, — Bible, — and Missionary Funds, I took it all for them. This brother knew nothing about our work, when he came three days since to Bristol. Thus the Lord, to show His continued care over us, raises up new helpers. They that trust in the Lord shall never be confounded! Some who helped for a while may fall asleep in Jesus; others may grow cold in the service of the Lord; others may be as desirous as ever to help, but have no longer the means; others may have both a willing heart to help, and have also the means, but may see it the Lord's will to lay them out in another way; — and thus, from one cause or another, were we to lean upon man, we should surely be confounded; but, in leaning upon the living God alone, we are BEYOND *disappointment, and* BEYOND *being forsaken because of death,* or *want of means,* or *want of love,* or *because of the claims of other work.* How precious to have learned in any measure to stand with God alone in the world, and yet to be happy, and to know that surely no good thing shall be withheld from us whilst we walk uprightly!"

A GREAT SINNER CONVERTED

In his REVIEW OF THE YEAR 1841, Mr. Müeller writes: —
"During this year I was informed about the conversion of one of the very greatest sinners, that I ever heard of in all my service for the Lord. Repeatedly I fell on my knees with his wife, and asked the Lord for his conversion, when she came to me in the deepest distress of soul, on account of the most barbarous and cruel treatment that she received from him, in his bitter enmity against her for the Lord's sake, and because he could not provoke her to be in a passion, and *she would not* strike him again, and the like. At the time when it was at its worst I pleaded especially on his behalf the promise in Matthew 18:19: 'Again I say unto you, that if two of you shall agree on earth as touching anything that they shall ask, it shall be done for them of my father which is in heaven.' And now this awful persecutor is converted."

PRAYER FOR SPIRITUAL BLESSING AMONG THE SAINTS

"On May 25th, I began to ask the Lord for greater real spiritual prosperity among the saints, among whom I labour in Bristol, than there ever yet had been among them; and now I have to record to the praise of the Lord that truly He has answered this request; for, considering all things, at no period has there been more manifestation of grace and truth, and spiritual power among us, than there is now while I am writing this for the press (1845). Not that we have attained to what we might; we are far, very far from it; but the Lord has been very, very good to us, and we have most abundant cause for thanksgiving."

WITHHOLDING THE REPORT

"Dec. 9 [1841]. — Today came in for the Orphans by the sale of stockings 10s. 10d. — We are now brought to the close of the sixth year of this part of the work, *having only in hand the money which has been put by for the rent*; but during the whole of this year we have been supplied with all that was needed.

"During the last three years we had closed the accounts on this day, and had, a few days after, some public meetings, at which, for the benefit of the hearers, we stated how the Lord had dealt with us during the year, and the substance of what had been stated at these meetings was afterwards printed for the benefit of the church at large. This time, however, it appeared to us better to delay for a while both the public meetings and the publishing of the Report. Through grace we had learned to lean upon the Lord only, being assured, that, if we were never to speak or write one single word more about this work, yet should we be supplied with means, as long as He should enable us to depend on Himself alone. But whilst we neither had had those public meetings for the purpose of exposing our necessity, nor had had the account of the Lord's dealings with us published for the sake of working thereby upon the feelings of the readers, and thus inducing them to give money, but only that we might by our experience benefit other saints; yet it might have appeared to some that, in making known our circumstances, we were actuated by some such motives. What better proof, therefore, could we give of our depending upon the living God alone, and not upon public meetings or printed Reports, than that, *in the midst of our deep poverty,* instead of being glad for the time to have come when we could make known our circumstances, we still went on quietly for some time longer, without saying anything. We therefore determined, as we sought and still seek in this work to act for the profit of the saints generally, to delay both the public meetings and the Report for a few months. *Naturally* we should have been, of course, as glad as anyone to have exposed our poverty at that time; but *spiritually* we were unable to delight even then in the prospect of the increased benefit that might be derived by the church at large from our acting as we did.

* * *

"Dec. 18 Saturday morning. There is now the greatest need, and only 4d. in hand, which I found in the box at my house; yet I fully believe the Lord will supply us this day also with all that is required. — Pause a few moments, dear reader! Observe two things! We acted *for God* in delaying the public meetings and the publishing of the Report; but *God's way leads always into trial, so far as sight and sense are concerned. Nature* always will be tried *in God's ways.* The Lord was saying by this poverty, 'I will now see whether you truly lean upon me, and whether you truly look to me.' Of all the seasons that I had ever passed through since I had been living in this way, *up to that time,* I never knew any period in which my faith was tried so sharply, as during the four months from Dec. 12, 1841, to April 12, 1842. But observe further: We might even now have altered our minds with respect to the public meetings and publishing the Report; *for no one knew our determination, at this time,* concerning the point. Nay, on the contrary, we knew with what delight very many children of God were looking forward to receive further accounts. But the Lord kept us steadfast to the conclusion, at which we had arrived under His guidance."

"HE ABIDETH FAITHFUL"

Under the date Jan. 25, 1842, Mr. Müeller writes: —
"Perhaps, dear reader, you have said in your heart before you have read thus far: 'How would it be, suppose the funds for the Orphans were reduced to nothing, and those who are engaged in the work had nothing of their own to give, and a meal time were come, and you had no food for the children.'

"Thus indeed it may be, for our hearts are desperately wicked. If ever we should be so left to ourselves, as that either we depend no more upon the living God, or that 'we regard iniquity in our hearts,' then such a state of things, we have reason to believe, would occur. But so long as we shall be enabled to trust in the living God, and so long as, though falling short in every way of what we might be, and ought to be, we are at least kept from living in sin, such a state of things cannot occur. Therefore, dear reader, if you yourself walk with God, and if, on that account, His glory is dear to you, I affectionately and earnestly entrust you to beseech Him to uphold us; for how awful would be the disgrace brought upon His holy name if we, who have so publicly made our boast in Him, and have spoken well of Him, should be left to disgrace Him, either by unbelief in the hour of trial, or by a life of sin in other respects."

DELAYED BUT SURE

"March 9 [1842]. — At a time of the greatest need, both with regard to the Day-Schools and the Orphans, so much so that we could not have gone on any longer without help, I received this day £10 from a brother who lives near Dublin. The money was divided between the Day-Schools and the Orphan-Houses. The following little circumstance is to be noticed respecting this donation: — As our need was so great, and my soul was, through grace, truly waiting upon the Lord, I looked out for supplies in the course of this morning. The post, however, was out, and no supplies had come. This did not in the least discourage me. I said to myself, the Lord can send means without the post, or even now, though the post is out, by this very delivery of letters He may have sent means, though the money is not yet in my hands. It was not long after I had thus spoken to myself, when, according to my hope in God, we were helped; for the brother who sent us the £10, had this time directed his letter to the Boys' Orphan-House, whence it was sent to me."

"LIKE AS A FATHER"

"March 17. — From the 12th to the 16th had come in £4 5s. 11 ½d. for the Orphans. This morning our poverty, which now has lasted more or less for several months, had become exceedingly great. I left my house a few minutes after seven to go to the Orphan-House, to see whether there was money enough to take in the milk, which is brought about eight o'clock. On my way it was specially my request that the Lord would be pleased to pity us, even as a father pitieth his children, and that He would not lay more upon us than He would enable us to bear, I especially entreated Him that He would now be pleased to refresh our hearts by sending us help. I likewise reminded Him of the consequences that would result, both in reference to believers and unbelievers, if we should have to give up the work because of want of means, and that He therefore would not permit of its coming to nought. I moreover again confessed before the Lord that I deserved not that He should continue to use me in this work any longer. While I was thus in prayer, about two minutes' walk from the Orphan-Houses, I met a brother who was going at this early hour to his business. After having exchanged a few words with him, I went on; but he presently ran after me, and gave me £1 for the Orphans. Thus the Lord speedily answered my prayer. Truly, it is worth being poor and greatly tried in faith, for the sake of having day by day such precious proofs of the loving interest which our kind Father takes in everything that concerns us. And how should our Father do otherwise? He that has given us the greatest possible proof of His love which He could have done, in giving us His own Son, surely He will with Him also freely give us all things."

TRUST IN THE LORD BETTER THAN MAN'S PROMISES

"May 6 [1845]. — About six weeks ago intimation was kindly given by a brother that he expected a certain considerable sum of money, and that, if he obtained it, a certain portion of it should be given to the Lord, so that £100 of it should be used for the work in my hands, and the other part for Brother Craik's and my own personal expenses. However, day after day passed away, and the money did not come. I did not trust in this money, yet, as during all this time, with scarcely any exception, we were more or less needy, I thought again and again about this brother's promise; though I did not, by the grace of God, trust in the brother who had made it, but in the Lord. Thus week after week passed away, and the money did not come. Now this morning it came to my mind, that such promises ought to be valued, in a certain sense, as nothing, *i.e.*, that the mind ought never for a moment to be directed to them, but to the living God, and to the living God only. I saw that such promises ought not to be of the value of one farthing, so far as it regards thinking about them for help. I therefore asked the Lord, when, as usual, I was praying with my beloved wife about the work in my hands that He would be pleased to take this whole matter, about that promise, completely out of my mind, and to help me, not to value it in the least, yea, to treat it as if not worth one farthing, but to keep my eye directed only to Himself. I was enabled to do so. We have not yet finished praying when I received the following letter:

May 5, 1845

Beloved Brother,

Are your bankers still Messrs. Stuckey and Co. of Bristol, and are their bankers still Messrs. Robarts and Co. of London? Please to instruct me on this; and if the case should be so, please to regard this as a letter of advice that £70 are paid to Messrs. Robarts and Co., for Messrs. Stuckey and Co., for you. This sum apply as the Lord may give you wisdom. I shall not send to Robarts and Co. until I hear from you.

Ever affectionately yours,

* * * *

"Thus the Lord rewarded at once this determination to endeavour not to look in the least to that promise from a brother, but only to Himself. But this was not all. About two o'clock this afternoon I received from the brother, who had more than forty days ago, made that promise, £166 18s., as he this day received the money, on the strength of which he had made that promise. Of this sum £100 are to be used for the work in my hands, and the remainder for brother Craik's and my own personal expenses."

Under date 1842 Mr. Müeller writes: —

"I desire that all the children of God, who may read these details, may thereby be lead to increased and more simple confidence in God for everything which they may need under any circumstances, and that these many answers to prayer may encourage them to pray, particularly as it regards the conversion of their friends and relatives, their own progress in grace and knowledge, the state of the saints whom they may know personally, the state of the church of God at large, and the success of the preaching of the Gospel. Especially I affectionately warn them against being led away by the device of Satan, to think that these things are peculiar to me, and cannot be enjoyed by all the children of God; for though, as has been stated before, every believer is not called upon to establish Orphan-Houses, Charity Schools, etc., and trust in the Lord for means; yet all believers are called upon, in the simple confidence of faith, to cast all their burdens upon Him, to trust in Him for everything, and not only to make every thing a subject of prayer, but to expect answers to their petitions which they have asked according to His will, and in the name of the Lord Jesus. — Think not, dear reader, that I have *the gift of faith,* that is, that gift of which we read in I Cor. 12:9, and which is mentioned along with 'the gifts of healing,' 'the working of miracles,' 'prophecy,' and that on that account I am able to trust in the Lord. *It is true* that the faith, which I am enabled to exercise, is altogether God's own gift; it is true that He alone supports it, and that He alone can increase it; it is true that, moment by moment, I depend upon Him for it, and that, if I were only one moment left to myself, my faith would utterly fail; but *it is not true* that my faith is that gift of faith which is spoken of in I Cor. 12:9 for the following reasons: —

"1. The faith which I am enabled to exercise with reference to the Orphan-Houses and my own temporal necessities, is not that 'faith' of which it is said in I Cor. 13:2 (evidently in allusion to the faith spoken of in I Cor. 12:9), 'Though I have all faith, so that I could remove mountains, and have not charity (love), I am nothing'; but it is the self-same faith which is found in *every believer,* and the growth of which I am most sensible of to myself; for, by little and little, it has been increasing for the last sixty-nine years.

"2. This faith which is exercised respecting the Orphan-Houses and my own temporal necessities, shows itself in the same measure, for instance, concerning the following points: I have never been permitted to doubt during the last sixty-nine years that my sins are forgiven, that I am a child of God, that I am beloved of God, and that I shall be finally saved; because I am enabled, by the grace of God, to exercise faith upon the word of God, and believe what God says in those passages which settle these matters (I John 5:1 — Gal. 3:26 — Acts 10:43 — Romans 10:9, 10 — John 3:16, etc.) . . . Further, when sometimes all has been dark, exceedingly dark, with reference to my service among the saints, judging from natural appearances; yea, when I should have been overwhelmed indeed in grief and despair, had I looked at things after the outward appearance; at such times I have sought to encourage myself in God, by laying hold in faith on His mighty power, His unchangeable love, and His infinite wisdom, and I have said to myself: God is able and willing to deliver me, if it be good for me; for it is written: 'He that spared not His own Son, but delivered Him up for us all, how shall He not with Him also freely give us all things?' Rom. 8:32. This, this it was which, being believed by me through grace, kept my soul in peace. — Further, when in connection with the Orphan-Houses, Day Schools, etc., trials have come upon me which were far heavier than the want of means when lying reports were spread that the Orphans had not enough to eat, or that they were cruelly treated in other respects, and the like; or when other trials, still greater, but which I cannot mention, have befallen me in connexion with this work, and that at a time when I was nearly a thousand miles absent from Bristol, and had to remain absent week after week: at such times my soul was stayed upon God; I believed His word of promise which was applicable to such cases; I poured out my soul before God, and arose from my knees in peace, because the trouble that was in the soul was in believing prayer cast upon God, and thus I was kept in peace, though I saw it to be the will of God to remain far away from the work. — Further, when I needed houses, fellow-labourers, masters and mistresses for the Orphans or for the Day Schools, I have been enabled to look for all to the Lord and trust in Him for help. — Dear reader, I may seem to boast; but, by the grace of God, I do not boast in thus speaking. From my inmost soul I do ascribe it to God alone that He has enabled me to trust in Him, and that hitherto He has not suffered my confidence in Him to fail. But I thought it needful to make these remarks, lest anyone should think that my depending upon God was a particular gift given to me, which other saints have no right to look for; or lest it should be thought that this my depending upon Him had *only to do with the obtaining of* MONEY *by prayer and faith*. By the grace of God I desire that my faith in God should extend towards EVERY thing, the smallest of my own temporal and spiritual concerns, and the smallest of the temporal and spiritual concerns of my family, towards the saints among whom I labour, the church at large, everything that has to do with the temporal and spiritual prosperity of the Scriptural Knowledge Institution, etc.

Dear reader, do not think that I have attained in faith (and how much less in other respects!) to that degree to which I might and ought to attain; but thank God for the faith which He has given me, and ask Him to uphold and increase it. And lastly, once more, let not Satan deceive you in making you think that you could not have the same faith but that it is only for persons who are situated as I am. When I lose such a thing as a key, I ask the Lord to direct me to it, and I look for an answer to my prayer; when a person with whom I have made an appointment does not come, according to the fixed time, and I begin to be inconvenienced by it, I ask the Lord to be pleased to hasten him to me and I look for an answer; when I do not understand a passage of the word of God, I lift up my heart to the Lord, that He would be pleased, by His Holy spirit to instruct me, and I expect to be taught, though I do not fix the time when, and the manner how it should be; when I am going to minister in the Word, I seek help from the Lord, and while I, in the consciousness of natural inability as well as utter unworthiness begin this His service, I am not cast down, but of good cheer, because I look for His assistance, and believe that He, for His dear Son's sake will help me. And thus in other of my temporal and spiritual concerns I pray to the Lord, and expect an answer to my requests; and may not you do the same, dear believing reader? Oh! I beseech you, do not think me an extraordinary believer, having privileges above other of God's dear children, which they cannot have; nor look on my way of acting as something that would not do for other believers. Make but trial! Do but stand still in the hour of trial, and you will see the help of God, if you trust in Him. But there is so often a forsaking the ways of the Lord in the hour of trial, and thus the *food of faith*, the means whereby our faith may be increased, is lost. This leads me to the following important point. You ask, How may I, a true believer, have my faith strengthened? The answer is this: —

"I. — Every good gift and every perfect gift is from above, and cometh down from the Father of lights, with whom is no variableness, neither shadow of turning." James 1:17. As the increase of faith is a good gift, it must come from God, and therefore He ought to be asked for this blessing.

"II. — The following means, however, ought to be used: — 1. *The careful reading of the word of God, combined with meditation on it.* Through reading of the word of God, and especially through meditation on the

word of God, the believer becomes more and more acquainted with the nature and character of God, and thus sees more and more, besides His holiness and justice, what a kind, loving, gracious, merciful, mighty, wise, and faithful Being He is, and, therefore, in poverty, affliction of body, bereavement in his family, difficulty in his service, want of a situation or employment, he will repose upon the *ability* of God to help him, because he has not only learned from His word that He is of almighty power and infinite wisdom, but he has also seen instance upon instance in the Holy Scriptures in which His almighty power and infinite wisdom have been actually exercised in helping and delivering His people; and he will repose upon the *willingness* of God to help him, because he has not only learned from the Scriptures what a kind, good, merciful, gracious, and faithful being God is, but because he has also seen in the word of God how, in a great variety of instances He has proved Himself to be so. And the consideration of this, if *God has become known to us through* prayer and meditation on His own word, will lead us, in general at least, with a measure of confidence to rely upon Him: and thus the reading of the word of God, together with meditation on it, will be one especial means to strengthen our faith.
2. As with reference to the growth of every grace of the Spirit, it is of the utmost importance that we seek to maintain an upright heart and a good conscience, and, therefore, do not knowingly and habitually indulge in those things which are contrary to the mind of God, so it is also particularly the case with reference to the *growth in faith*. How can I possibly continue to act faith upon God, concerning anything, if I am habitually grieving Him, and seek to detract from the glory and honour of Him in whom I profess to trust, upon whom I profess to depend? All my confidence toward God, all my leaning upon Him in the hour of trial will be gone, if I have a guilty conscience, and do not seek to put away this guilty conscience, but still continue to do the things which are contrary to the mind of God. And if, in any particular instance, I cannot trust in God, because of the guilty conscience, then my faith is weakened by that instance of distrust; for faith with every fresh trial of it either increases by trusting God, and thus getting help, or it decreases by not trusting Him; and then there is less and less power of looking simply and directly to Him, and a habit of self-dependence is begotten or encouraged. One or the other of these will always be the case in each particular instance. Either we trust in God, and in that case we neither

trust in ourselves, nor in our fellow-men, nor in circumstances, nor in anything besides; or we DO trust in one or more of these, and in that case do NOT trust in God. 3. If we, indeed, desire our faith to be strengthened, we should not shrink from opportunities where our faith may be tried, and, therefore, through the trial, be strengthened. In our natural state we dislike dealing with God alone. Through our natural alienation from God we shrink from Him, and from eternal realities. This cleaves to us more or less, even after our regeneration. Hence it is, that more or less, even as believers, we have the same shrinking from standing with God alone, — from depending upon Him alone, — from looking to Him alone: —and yet this is the very position in which we ought to be, if we wish our faith to be strengthened. The more I am in a position to be tried in faith with reference to my body, my family, my service for the Lord, my business, etc., the more shall I have opportunity of seeing God's help and deliverance; and every fresh instance, in which He helps and delivers me, will tend towards the increase of my faith. On this account, therefore, the believer shall not shrink from situations, positions, circumstances, in which his faith may be tried; but should cheerfully embrace them as opportunities where he may see the hand of God stretched out on his behalf, to help and deliver him, and whereby he may thus have his faith strengthened. 4. The last important point for the strengthening of our faith is, that we let God work for us, when the hour of the trial of our faith comes, and do not work a deliverance of our own. Wherever God has given faith, it is given, among other reasons, for the very purpose of being tried.

"Yea, however weak our faith may be, God will try it; only with this restriction, that as in every way, He leads on gently, gradually, patiently, so also with reference to the trial of our faith. At first our faith will be tried very little in comparison with what it may be afterwards; for God never lays more upon us that He is willing to enable us to bear. Now when the trial of faith comes, we are naturally inclined to distrust God, and to trust rather in ourselves, or in our friends, or in circumstances.

"We will rather work a deliverance of our own somehow or other, than simply look to God and wait for His help. But if we do not patiently wait for God's help, if we work a deliverance of our own, then at the next trial of our faith it will be thus again, we shall be again inclined to deliver ourselves; and thus with every fresh instance of that kind, our faith will decrease; whilst on the contrary, were we to stand still, in order to see the salvation of God, to see His hand stretched out on our behalf, trusting in Him alone, then our faith would be increased, and with every fresh case in which the hand of God is stretched out on our behalf in the hour of the trial of our faith, our faith would be increased yet more.

"Would the believer, therefore, have his faith strengthened, he must especially, *give time to God*, who tries his faith in order to prove to His child, in the end, how willing He is to help and deliver him, the moment it is good for him."

In the early years of the Institution Mr. Müeller and his fellow labourers had to endure many severe trials of faith, as some of these instances show.

Mr. Müeller when writing of this period says: —

"Though now (July, 1845) for about seven years our funds have been so exhausted, that it has been a *rare* case that there have been means in hand to meet the necessities of more than 100 persons for *three days* together; yet I have been only once tried in spirit, and that was on September 18, 1838, when, for the first time the Lord seemed not to regard our prayer. But when He did send help at that time, and I saw that it was only for the trial of our faith, and because He had not forsaken the work, that we were brought so low, my soul was so strengthened and encouraged, that I have not only not been allowed to distrust the Lord, but *I have not been even cast down when in the deepest poverty* since that time."

A GIFT OF £12

"Aug. 20 [1838]. — The £5 which I had received on the 18th, had been given for housekeeping, so that to-day I was again penniless. But my eyes were up to the Lord. I gave myself to prayer this morning, knowing that I should want again this week at least £13, if not above £20. To-day I received £12 in answer to prayer, from a lady who is staying at Clifton, whom I had never seen before. Adorable Lord, grant that this may be a fresh encouragement to me!"

A SOLEMN CRISIS

Regarding one of the sharpest times of trial Mr. Müeller writes: —

"Sept. 10 [1838]. Monday morning. Neither Saturday nor yesterday had any money come in. It appeared to me now needful to take some steps on account of our need, *i.e.*, to go to the Orphan-Houses, call the brethren and sisters together, (who, except brother T____, had never been informed about the state of the funds), state the case to them, see how much money was needed for the present, tell them that amidst all this trial of faith I still believed that God would help, and to pray with them. Especially, also, I mean to go for the sake of telling them that no more articles must be purchased than we have the means to pay for, but to let there be nothing lacking in any way to the children as it regards nourishing food and needful clothing; for I would rather at once send them away than that they should lack. I meant to go for the sake also of seeing whether there were still articles remaining which had been sent for the purpose of being sold, or whether there were any articles really needless, that we might turn them into money. I felt that the matter was now come to a solemn crisis. About half-past nine sixpence came in, which had been put anonymously into the box at Gideon Chapel. This money seems to me like an earnest, that God would have compassion and send more. About ten, after I had returned from brother Craik, to whom I had unbosomed my heart again, whilst once more in prayer for help, a sister called who gave two sovereigns to my wife for the Orphans, stating that she had felt herself stirred up to come and that she had delayed coming already too long. A few minutes after, when I went into the room where she was, she gave me two sovereigns more, and all this without knowing the least about our need. Thus the Lord most mercifully has sent us a little help, to the great encouragement of my faith. A few minutes after I was called on for money from the Infant Orphan-House, to which I sent £2, and £1, 0s. 6d. to the Boys' Orphan-House, and £1 to the Girls' Orphan-House."

A PRECIOUS DELIVERANCE

"Sept. 17 [1838]. — The trial still continues. It is now more and more trying, even to faith, as each day comes. Truly, the Lord has wise purposes in allowing us to call so long upon Him for help. But I am sure God will send help, if we can but wait. One of the labourers had had a little money come in of which he gave 12s. 6d.; another labourer gave 11s. 8d., being all the money she had left; this, with 17s. 6d., which, partly, had come in, and, partly was in hand, enabled us to pay what needed to be paid, and to purchase provisions, so that nothing yet, in any way, has been lacking. This evening I was rather tired respecting the long delay of larger sums coming; but being led to go to the Scriptures for comfort, my soul was greatly refreshed, and my faith again strengthened, by the 34th Psalm, so that I went very cheerfully to meet with my dear fellow-labourers for prayer. I read to them the Psalm, and sought to cheer their hearts through the precious promises contained in it."

"Sept. 18. — Brother T. had 25s. in hand, and I had 3s. This £1 8s. enabled us to buy the meat and bread, which was needed; a little tea for one of the houses, and milk for all; no more than this is needed. Thus the Lord has provided not only for this day; for there is bread for two days in hand. Now, however, we are come to an extremity. The funds are exhausted. The labourers, who had a little money, have given as long as they had any left. Now observe how the Lord helped us! A lady from the neighbourhood of London who brought a parcel with money from her daughter, arrived four or five days since in Bristol, and took lodgings next door to the Boys' Orphan-House. This afternoon she herself kindly brought me the money, amounting to £3 2s. 6d. We had been reduced so low as to be on the point of selling those things which could be spared; but this morning I had asked the Lord, if it might be, to prevent the necessity, of our doing so. That the money had been so near the Orphan-Houses for several days without being given, is a plain proof that it was from the beginning in the heart of God to help us; but because He delights in the prayers of His children, He had allowed us to pray so long; also to try our faith, and to make the answer so much the sweeter. It is indeed a precious deliverance. I burst out into loud praises and thanks the first moment I was alone, after I had received the money. I met with my fellow-labourers again this evening for prayer and praise; their hearts were not a little cheered. This money was this evening divided, and will comfortably provide for all that will be needed to-morrow."

Chapter II
THE NEW ORPHAN HOUSES, ASHLEY DOWN

A COMPLAINT having been received from a gentleman in October, 1845, that some of the inhabitants of Wilson Street were inconvenienced by the Orphan-Houses being in that street, Mr. Müeller ultimately decided for that and other reasons, after much prayerful meditation, to build an Orphan-House elsewhere to accommodate 300 children, and commenced to ask the Lord for means for so doing: —

"Jan. 31 [1846]. — It is now 89 days since I have been daily waiting upon God about the building of an Orphan-House. The time seems to me now near when the Lord will give us a piece of ground, and I told the brethren and sisters so this evening after our usual Saturday evening prayer meeting at the Orphan-Houses.

"Feb. 1. — A poor widow sent to-day 10s.

"Feb. 2. — To-day I heard of suitable and cheap land on Ashley Down.

"Feb. 3. — Saw the land. It is the most desirable of all I have seen. — There was anonymously put in an Orphan-box at my house a sovereign, in a piece of paper, on which was written, 'The New Orphan-House.'

"Feb. 4. — This evening I called on the owner of the land on Ashley Down, about which I had heard on the 2nd, but he was not at home. As I, however, had been informed that I should find him at his house of business, I went there, but did not find him there either, as he had *just before* left. I might have called again at his residence, at a later hour, having been informed by one of the servants that he would be sure to be at home about eight o'clock; but I did not do so, judging that there was the hand of God in my not finding him at either place: and I judged it best therefore not to force the matter, but to 'let patience have her perfect work.'

"Feb. 5. — Saw this morning the owner of the land. He told me that he awoke at three o'clock this morning and could not sleep again till five. While he was thus lying awake, his mind was all the time occupied about the piece of land, respecting which inquiry had been made of him for the building of an Orphan-House, at my request; and he determined that if I should apply for it, he would not only let me have it, but for £120 per acre, instead of £200; the price which he had previously asked for it. How good is the Lord! The agreement was made this morning, and I purchased a field of nearly seven acres, at £120 per acre.

"Observe the hand of God in my not finding the owner at home last evening! The Lord meant to speak to His servant first about this matter, during a sleepless night, and to lead him *fully* to decide, before I had seen him."

"BECAUSE OF HIS IMPORTUNITY"

"Nov. 19 [1846]. — I am now led more and more to importune the Lord to send me the means, which are requisite in order that I may be able to commence the building. Because (1) it has been for some time past publicly stated in print, that I allow it is not without ground that some of the inhabitants of Wilson Street consider themselves inconvenienced by the Orphan-Houses being in that street, and I long therefore to be able to remove the Orphans from thence as soon as possible. (2) I become more and more convinced, that it would be greatly for the benefit of the children, both physically and morally, with God's blessing, to be in such a position as they are intended to occupy, when the New Orphan-House shall have been built. And (3) because the number of very poor and destitute Orphans, that are waiting for admission, is so great, and there are constantly fresh applications made. Now whilst, by God's grace, I would not wish the building to be begun one single day sooner than is His will; and whilst I firmly believe, that He will give me, in His own time every shilling which I need; yet I also know, that He delights in being earnestly entreated, and that He takes pleasure in the continuance in prayer, and in the importuning Him, which so clearly is to be seen from the parable of the widow and the unjust judge. Luke 18:1-8. For these reasons I gave myself again particularly to prayer last evening, that the Lord would send further means, being also especially led to do so, in addition to the above reasons, because there had come in but little comparatively, since the 29th of last month. This morning, between five and six o'clock I prayed again, among other points, about the Building Fund, and then had a long season for the reading of the word of God. In the course of my reading I came to Mark 11:24, 'What things soever ye desire, when ye pray, believe that ye receive them, and ye shall have them.' The importance of the truth contained in this portion I have often felt and spoken about; but this morning I felt it again most particularly, and, applying it to the New Orphan-House, said to the Lord: 'Lord, I believe that Thou wilt give me all I need for this work. I am sure that I shall have all, because I believe that I receive in answer to my prayer.' Thus, with the heart full of peace concerning this work, I went on to the other part of the chapter, and to the next chapter. After family prayer I had again my usual season for prayer with regard to all the many parts of the work, and the various necessities thereof, asking also blessings upon my fellow-labourers, upon the circulation of Bibles and Tracts, and upon the precious souls in the Adult School, the Sunday Schools, the Six Day Schools, and the four Orphan-Houses. Amidst all the many things I again made my requests about means for the Building. And now observe: About five minutes, after I had risen from my knees, there was given to me a registered letter, containing a cheque for £300, of which £280 are for the Building Fund, £10 for my own personal expenses, and £10 for Brother Craik. The Lord's holy name be praised for this precious encouragement, by which the Building Fund is now increased to more than six thousand pounds."

MR. MÜELLER'S FIRST ORPHAN-HOUSE

"Jan. 25 [1847]. — The season of the year is now approaching, when building may be begun. Therefore with increased earnestness I have given myself unto prayer, importuning the Lord that He would be pleased to appear on our behalf, and speedily send the remainder of the amount which is required, and I have increasingly, of late, felt that the time is drawing near, when the Lord will give me all that which is requisite for commencing the building. All the various arguments which I have often brought before God, I brought also again this morning before Him. It is now 14 months and 3 weeks since day by day I have uttered my petitions to God on behalf of this work. I rose from my knees this morning in full confidence, not only that God *could*, but

THE NEW ORPHAN HOUSES, ASHLEY DOWN 25

also *would*, send the means, and that soon. Never, during all these 14 months and 3 weeks, have I had the least doubt, that I should have all that which is requisite. — And now, dear believing reader, rejoice and praise with me. About an hour, after I had prayed thus, there was given to me the sum of Two Thousand Pounds for the Building Fund. Thus I have received altogether £9,285 3s. 9½d. towards this work. — I cannot describe the joy I had in God when I received this donation. It must be known from experience, in order to be felt. 447 days I have had day by day to wait upon God, before the sum reached the above amount. How great is the blessing which the soul obtains by *trusting in God*, and *by waiting patiently*. Is it not manifest how precious it is to carry on God's work in this way, even with regard to the obtaining of means?"

The total amount which came in for the Building Fund was £15,784 18s. 10d.

ORPHAN-HOUSES NOS. 2 & 3

"March 12, 1862. — It was in November, 1850, that my mind became exercised about enlarging the Orphan Work from 300 Orphans to 1000, and subsequently to 1150; and it was in June, 1851, that this my purpose became known, having kept it secret for more than seven months, whilst day by day praying about it. From the end of November, 1850, to this day, March 12, 1862, not one single day has been allowed to pass, without this contemplated enlargement being brought before God in prayer, and generally more than once a day. But only now, this day, the New Orphan-House No. 3 was so far advanced, that it could be opened. Observe then, first, esteemed Reader, how long it may be before a full answer to our prayers, even to thousands and tens of thousands of prayers, is granted; yea, though those prayers may be believing prayers, earnest prayers, and offered up in the name of the Lord Jesus, and though we may only for the sake of the honour of our Lord desire the answer: for I did, by the grace of God, without the least doubt and wavering look for more than eleven years for the full answer; * * * and I sought only in this matter the glory of God."

PRAYING THREE TIMES DAILY FOR HELPERS

"As in the case of No. 2, so also in the case of the New Orphan-House

No. 3, I had daily prayed for the needed helpers and assistants for the various departments. Before a stone was laid, I began to pray for this; and, as the building progressed, I continued day by day to bring this matter before God, feeling assured, that, as in everything else, so in this particular also, He would graciously be pleased to appear on our behalf and help us, as the whole work is intended for His honour and glory.

"At last the time was near when the house could be opened, and the time therefore near when the applications, which had been made in writing during more than two years previously, should be considered, for the filling up of the various posts. It now, however, was found that, whilst there had been about 50 applications made for the various situations, some places could not be filled up, because either the individuals, who had applied for them, were married, or were, on examination, found unsuitable. This was no small trial of faith; for day by day, for years, had I asked God to help me in this particular, even as He had done in the case of the New Orphan-House No. 2; I had also expected help, confidently expected help: and yet now, when help seemed needed, it was wanting. What was now to be done, dear Reader? Would it have been right to charge God with unfaithfulness? Would it have been right to distrust Him? Would it have been right to say, it is useless to pray? By no means. This, on the contrary, I did; I thanked God for all the help, He had given me in connection with the whole of the enlargement; I thanked Him for enabling me to overcome so many and such great difficulties; I thanked Him for the helpers He had given me for No. 2; I thanked Him, also, for the helpers He had given me already for No. 3; and instead of distrusting God, I looked upon this delay of the full answer to prayer, only as a trial of faith, and therefore resolved, that, instead of praying *once* a day with my dear wife about this matter, as we had been doing day by day for years, we should now meet daily *three* times, to bring this before God. I also brought the matter before the whole staff of my helpers in the work requesting their prayers. Thus I have now continued for about four months longer in prayer, day by day calling upon God three times on account of this need, and the result has been, that one helper after another has been given, without the help coming *too* late, or the work getting into confusion; or the reception of the children being hindered; and I am fully assured, that the few who are yet needed will also be found, when they are *really* required."

THE NEW ORPHAN HOUSES, ASHLEY DOWN

DIFFICULTIES REMOVED AFTER PRAYER AND PATIENCE

Mr. Müeller relates the following incidents in connection with the purchase of the land for the Fourth and Fifth Orphan-Houses, after receiving five thousand pounds for the Building Fund:

"I had now, through all that had come in since May 26th, 1864, including this last-mentioned donation, above Twenty-Seven Thousand Pounds in hand. I had patiently waited God's time. I had determined to do nothing, until I had the full half of the sum needed for the two houses. But now, having above Two Thousand Pounds beyond the half, I felt, after again seeking counsel from God, quite happy, in taking steps for the purchase of the land.

"My eyes had been for years directed to a beautiful piece of land, only separated by the turnpike road from the ground on which the New Orphan-House No. 3 is erected. The land is about 18 acres, with a small house and outhouses built on one end thereof. Hundreds of times had I prayed, within the last years, that God for Jesus' sake would count me worthy, to be allowed to erect on this ground two more Orphan-Houses; and hundreds of times I had with a prayerful eye looked on this land, yea, as it were, bedewed it with my prayers. I might have bought it years ago; but that would have been going before the Lord. I had money enough in hand to have paid for it years ago; but I desired patiently, submissively, to wait God's own time, and for Him to mark it clearly and distinctly that His time was come, and that I took the step according to His will; for whatever I might apparently accomplish, if the work were mine, and not the Lord's, I could expect no blessing. But now the Lord's mind was clearly and distinctly made manifest. I had enough money in hand to pay for the land and to build one house, and therefore I went forward, after having still asked the Lord for guidance, and being assured that it was His will I should take active steps. The first thing I did was, to see the agent who acted for the owner of the land, and to ask him, whether the land was for sale. He replied that it was, but that it was let till March 25th, 1867. He said that he would write for the price. Here a great difficulty at once presented itself, that the land was let for two years and four months longer, whilst it appeared desirable that I should be able to take possession of it in about six months, viz., as soon as the conveyance could be made out, and the plans be ready for the New Orphan-House No. 4, and arrangements be made with contractors. But I was not discouraged by this difficulty; for I expected, through prayer, to make happy and satisfactory arrangements with the tenant, being willing to give him a fair compensation for leaving before his time had expired. But, before I had time to see about this, two other great difficulties presented themselves: the one was, that the owner asked £7,000 for the land, which I judged to be considerably more than its value; and the other, that I heard that the Bristol Waterworks Company intended to make an additional reservoir for their water, on this very land, and to get an Act of Parliament passed to that effect.

"Pause here for a few moments, esteemed Reader. You have seen, how the Lord brought me so far, with regard to pecuniary means, that I felt now warranted to go forward; and I may further add, that I was brought to this point as the result of thousands of times praying regarding this object; and that there were, also, many hundreds of children waiting for admission; and yet, after the Lord Himself so manifestly had appeared on our behalf, by the donation of £5,000, He allows this apparent death-blow to come upon the whole. But thus I have found it hundreds of times since I have known the Lord. The difficulties, which He is pleased to allow to arise, are only allowed, under such circumstances, for the exercise of our faith and patience; and more prayer, more patience, and the exercise of faith, will remove the difficulties. Now, as I knew the Lord, these difficulties were no insurmountable difficulties to me, for I put my trust in Him, according to that word: 'The Lord also will be a refuge for the oppressed, a refuge in times of trouble. And they that know Thy name will put their trust in Thee: for Thou, Lord, hast not forsaken them that seek Thee.' (Psalm 9:9, 10). I gave myself, therefore, earnestly to prayer concerning all these three especial difficulties which had arisen regarding the land. I prayed several times daily about the matter, and used the following means: 1. I saw the Acting Committee of the Directors of the Bristol Waterworks Company regarding their intended reservoir on the land, which I was about to purchase, and stated to them, what I had seen in print concerning their intentions. They courteously stated to me, that only a small portion of the land would be required, not enough to interfere with my purpose; and that, if it could be avoided, even this small portion should not be taken. 2. This being settled, I now saw the tenant, after many prayers; for I desired, as a Christian, that if this land were bought, it should be done under amicable circumstances with regard to him. At the first interview, I stated my intentions to him, at the same time expressing my desire that the matter should be settled pleasantly with regard to himself. He said that he would consider the matter, and desired a few days for that purpose. After a week I saw him again, and he then kindly stated, that, as the land was wanted for such an object, he would not stand in the way; but that, as he had laid out a good deal on the house and land, he expected a compensation for leaving it before his time was up. As I, of course, was quite willing to give a *fair* and *reasonable* compensation, I considered this a very precious answer to prayer. 3. I now entered upon the third difficulty, the price of the land. I knew well how much the land was worth to the Orphan Institution; but its value to the Institution was not the market value. I gave myself, therefore, day by day to prayer, that the Lord would constrain the owner to accept a considerably lower sum than he had asked; I also pointed out to him why it was not worth as much as he asked. At last he consented to take £5,500 instead of £7,000, and I accepted the offer; for I knew by the level character of the land we should save a considerable sum for the two houses, and that by the new sewer, which only a few months before had been completed, running along under the turnpike road near the field, we should be considerably benefited. In addition to these two points I had to take into the account, that we can have gas from Bristol, as in the three houses already in operation. And lastly, the most important point of all, the nearness of this piece of land to the other three houses, so that all could easily be under the same direction and superintendence. In fact, no other piece of land, near or far off, would present so much advantage to us, as this spot, which the Lord thus so very kindly had given to us. All being now settled, I proceeded to have the land conveyed to the same trustees who stood trustees for the New Orphan-Houses No. 1, No. 2, and No. 3. — I have thus minutely dwelt on these various matters for the encouragement of the reader, that he may not be discouraged by difficulties, however great and many and varied, but give himself to prayer, trusting in the Lord for help, yea, expecting help, which, in His own time and way, He will surely grant."

ORPHAN-HOUSES NOS. 4 & 5

"March 5, 1874. — Both houses, No. 4 and No. 5, have now been for years in operation, No. 4 since Nov. 1868 and No. 5 since the beginning of the year 1870, and above 1,200 Orphans have been already received into them, and month after month more are received, as the Orphans are sent out from them as apprentices or servants. Moreover all the expenses in connection with their being built, fitted up and furnished were met to the full, as the demands arose, and, after all had been paid, there was left a balance of several thousand pounds, which is being used for keeping the houses in repair. See, esteemed Reader, how abundantly God answered our prayers, and how plain it is, that we were not mistaken, after we had patiently and prayerfully sought to ascertain His will. Be encouraged, therefore, yet further and further to confide in the Living God."

Chapter III
PRECIOUS ANSWERS TO PRAYER

IN REMARKABLE WAYS God helped Mr. Müeller as "The Narratives" show: —

THE ARTIST'S FIRST RETURN

"April 30 [1859]. — Received the following letter from a considerable distance: 'My dear Christian Brother, I am the husband of Mrs. ____ who sends you by this post the two Sovereign pieces. How can we better dispose of this relic of affectionate remembrance, than by depositing it in the bank of Christ, who always pays the best interest, and never fails. — Now, my best and spiritual counsellor, I cannot express to you the exceeding great joy I feel, in relating what follows. I am an artist, a *poor* artist, a landscape painter. About two weeks ago I sent a picture to Bristol for exhibition, just as I finished your book that was lent us. I most humbly and earnestly prayed to God to enable me, by the sale of my Bristol picture, to have the blessed privilege of sending you *half the proceeds*. The price of the picture is £20. Now mark. Immediately the exhibition is open, God, in His mercy, mindful of my prayer, sends me a purchaser. I have exhibited in Bristol before, *but never sold* a picture. Oh! my dear friend, my very heart leaps for joy. I have never been so near God before. Through your instrumentality I have been enabled to draw nearer to God, with more earnestness, more faith, more holy desires. — This is the *first return* God has blessed me with for the whole of my last year's labours. What a blessing to have it so returned! — Oh, with what joy I read your book! — The picture I speak of is now being exhibited in the academy of arts in Clifton, numbered in the Catalogue —, the title is ____. I cannot pay you till the close of the exhibition, as I shall not be paid till then, &C.' Of such letters I have had thousands during the last 40 years."

THE NORTH WIND CHANGED INTO A SOUTH WIND

"It was towards the end of November of 1857, when I was most unexpectedly informed that the boiler of our heating apparatus at No. 1 leaked very considerably, so that it was impossible to go through the winter with such a leak. — Our heating apparatus consists of a large cylinder boiler, inside of which the fire is kept, and with which boiler the water pipes, that warm the rooms, are connected. Hot air is also connected with this apparatus. The boiler had been considered suited for the work of the winter. To suspect that it was worn out, and not to do anything towards replacing it by a new one, and to have said, I will trust in God regarding it, would be careless presumption, but not faith in God. It would be the counterfeit of faith.

"The boiler is entirely surrounded by brickwork; its state, therefore, could not be known without taking down the brickwork; this, if needless, would be rather injurious to the boiler, than otherwise; and as for eight winters we had had no difficulty in this way, we had not anticipated it now. But suddenly, and most unexpectedly, at the commencement of the winter, this difficulty occurred. What then was to be done? For the children, especially the younger infants, I felt deeply concerned, that they might not suffer, through want of warmth. But how were we to obtain warmth? The introduction of a *new* boiler would, in all probability, take many weeks. The *repairing* of the boiler was a questionable matter, on account of the greatness of the leak; but, if not, nothing could be said of it, till the brick-chamber in which it is enclosed, was at least in part, removed; but that would, at least, as far as we could judge, take days; and what was to be done in the meantime, to find warm rooms for 300 children? It naturally occurred to me, to introduce temporary gas-stoves; but on further weighing the matter, it was found, that we should be unable to heat our very large rooms with gas, except we had many stoves, which we could not introduce, as we had not a sufficient quantity of gas to spare from our lighting apparatus. Moreover, for each of these stoves we needed a small chimney, to carry off the impure air. This mode of heating, therefore, though applicable to a hall, a staircase, or a shop, would not suit our purpose. I also thought of the temporary introduction of Arnott's stoves; but they would have been unsuitable, requiring long chimneys (as they would have been of a temporary kind) to go out of the windows. On this account, the uncertainty of their answering in our case, and the disfigurement of the rooms, led me to give up this plan also. But what was to be done? Gladly would I have paid £100, if thereby the difficulty could have been overcome, and the children not be exposed to suffer for many days from being in cold rooms. At last I determined on falling entirely into the hands of God, who is very merciful and of tender compassion, and I decided on having the brick-chamber opened, to see the extent of the damage, and whether the boiler might be repaired, so as to carry us through the winter.

"The day was fixed, when the workmen were to come, and all the necessary arrangements were made. The fire, of course, had to be let out while the repairs were going on. But now see. After the day was fixed for the repairs a bleak North wind set in. It began to blow either on Thursday or Friday before the Wednesday afternoon, when the fire was to be let out. Now came the first really cold weather, which we had in the beginning of that winter, during the first days of December. What was to be done? The repairs could not be put off. I now asked the Lord for two things, viz., that He would be pleased to change the north wind into a south wind, and that He would give to the workmen 'a mind to work'; for I remembered how much Nehemiah accomplished in 52 days, whilst building the walls of Jerusalem, because 'the people had a mind to work.' Well, the memorable day came. The evening before, the bleak north wind blew still; but, on the Wednesday, the south wind blew: exactly as I had prayed. The weather was so mild that no fire was needed. The brickwork was removed, the leak is found out very soon, the boiler makers begin to repair in good earnest. About half-past eight in the evening, when I was going home, I was informed at the lodge, that the acting principal of the firm, whence the boiler makers came, had arrived to see how the work was going on, and whether he could in any way speed the matter. I went immediately, therefore, into the cellar, to see him with the men, to seek to expedite the business. In speaking to the principal of this, he said in their hearing, 'the men will work late this evening, and come very early again tomorrow.'

" 'We would rather, Sir,' said the leader, 'work all night.' Then remembered I the second part of my prayer, that God would give the men 'a mind to work.' Thus it was: by the morning the repair was accomplished, the leak was stopped, though with great difficulty, and within about 30 hours the brickwork was up again, and the fire in the boiler; and all the time the south wind blew so mildly, that there was not the least need of a fire.

"Here, then, is one of our difficulties which was overcome by prayer and faith."

CONVERSION OF THE ORPHANS

"May 26, 1860. — Day after day, and year after year, by the help of God, we labour in prayer for the spiritual benefit of the Orphans under our care. These our supplications, which have been for 24 years brought before the Lord concerning them, have been abundantly answered, in former years, in the conversion of hundreds from among them. We have, also, had repeated seasons in which, within a short time, or even all at once, *many* of the Orphans were converted. Such a season we had about three years since, when, within a few days, about 60 were brought to believe in the Lord Jesus; and such seasons we have had again twice during the first year. The first was in July, 1859, when the Spirit of God wrought so mightily in one school of 120 girls, as that very many, yea more than one-half, were brought under deep concern about the salvation of their souls. This work, moreover, was not a mere momentary excitement; but, after more than eleven months have elapsed, there are 31 concerning whom there is *full* confidence as to their conversion, and 32 concerning whom there is likewise a goodly measure of confidence, though not to the same amount, as regarding the 31. There are therefore 63 out of the 120 Orphans in that one School who are considered to have been converted in July, 1859. This blessed and mighty work of the Holy Spirit cannot be traced to any particular cause. It was however, a most precious answer to prayer. As such we look upon it, and are encouraged by it to further waiting upon God. The second season of the mighty working of the Holy Spirit among the Orphans, during the past year, was at the end of January and the beginning of February, 1860. The particulars of it are of the deepest interest; but I must content myself by stating, that this great work of the Spirit of God in January and February, 1860, began among the younger class of the children under our care, little girls of about 6, 7, 8 and 9 years old; then extended to the older girls; and then to the boys, so that within about 10 days above 200 of the Orphans were stirred up to be anxious about their souls, and in *many* instances found peace *immediately*, through faith in our Lord Jesus. They at once requested to be allowed to hold prayer-meetings among themselves, and have had these meetings ever since. Many of them also manifested a concern about the salvation of their companions and relations, and spoke or wrote to them, about the way to be saved."

APPRENTICING THE ORPHANS

"In the early part of the summer, 1862, it was found that we had several boys ready to be apprenticed; but there were no applications made by masters for apprentices. As all our boys are invariably sent out as indoor apprentices, this was no small difficulty; for we not only look for Christian masters, but consider their business, and examine into their position, to see whether they are suitable; and the master must also be willing to receive the apprentice into his own family. Under these circumstances, we again gave ourselves to prayer, as we have done for more than twenty years before, concerning this thing, instead of advertising, which, in all probability, would only bring before us masters who desire apprentices for the sake of the premium. We remembered how good the Lord had been to us, in having helped us hundreds of times before, in this very matter. Some weeks passed, but the difficulty remained. We continued, however, in prayer, and then one application was made, and then another; and since we first began to pray about this matter, last summer, we have been able to send out altogether 18 boys up to May 26, 1863; the difficulty was thus again entirely overcome by prayer, as every one of the boys, whom it was desirable to send out, has been sent out."

SICKNESS AT THE ORPHANAGE

Sickness at times visited the houses.

"During the summer and autumn of 1866 we had also the measles at all the three Orphan-Houses. After they had made their appearance, our especial prayer was: 1. That there might not be too many children ill at one time in this disease, so that our accommodation in the Infirmary rooms or otherwise might be sufficient. This prayer was answered to the full; for though we had at the New Orphan-House

No. 1 not less than 83 cases, in No. 2 altogether 111, and in No. 3 altogether 68; yet God so graciously was pleased to listen to our supplications, as that when our spare rooms were filled with the invalids, He so long stayed the spreading of the measles till a sufficient number were restored, so as to make room for others, who were taken ill. 2. Further we prayed, that the children, who were taken ill in the measles, might be safely brought through and not die. Thus it was. We had the full answer to our prayers; for though 262 children altogether had the measles, not one of them died. 3. Lastly we prayed, that no evil physical consequences might follow this disease, as is so often the case; this was also granted. All the 262 children not only recovered, but did well afterwards. I gratefully record this signal mercy and blessing of God, and this full and precious answer to prayer, to the honour of His name."

HELP FOR NEEDY BRETHREN

1863. — "The end of the year was now at hand, and, in winding up the accounts, it was my earnest desire, to do once more all I could, in sending help to needy labourers in the gospel. I went therefore through the list, writing against the various names of those to whom I had not already recently sent, what amount it appeared desirable to send; and I found, when these sums were added together, the total was £476, but £280 was all I had in hand. I wrote therefore a cheque for £280, though I would have gladly sent £476, yet felt thankful, at the same time, that I had this amount in hand for these brethren. Having written the cheque, as the last occupation of the day, then came my usual season for prayer, for the many things which I daily, by the help of God, bring before Him; and then again, I brought also the case of these preachers of the Gospel before the Lord, and besought Him that He would even now be pleased to give me yet a goodly sum for them, though there remained but three days to the close of our year. This being done, I went home about nine o'clock in the evening, and found there had arrived from a great distance £100 for Missions, with £100 left at my disposal, and £5 for myself. I took, therefore, the whole £200 for Missions, and thus had £480 in hand to meet the £476 which I desired for this object. Those who know the blessedness of really trusting in God, and getting help from Him, as in this case, in answer to prayer, will be able to enter into the spiritual enjoyment I had in the reception of that donation, in which both the answer to prayer was granted, and with it the great enjoyment of gladdening the hearts of many devoted servants of Christ."

THE HEART'S DESIRE GIVEN TO HELP MISSION WORK IN CHINA

"Sept. 30 [1869]. — From Yorkshire £50. — Received also One Thousand Pounds to-day for the Lord's work in China. About this donation it is especially to be noticed that for months it had been my earnest desire to do more than ever for Mission Work in China, and I had already taken steps to carry out this desire, when this donation of One Thousand Pounds came to hand. This precious answer to prayer for means should be a particular encouragement to all who are engaged in the Lord's work, and who may need means for it. It proves afresh, that, if our work is His work, and we honour Him, by waiting upon and looking to Him for means, He will surely, in His own time and way, supply them."

THE JOY OF ANSWERS TO PRAYER

"The joy which answers to prayer give, cannot be described; and the impetus which they afford to the spiritual life is exceedingly great. The experience of this happiness I desire for all my Christian readers. If you believe indeed in the Lord Jesus for the salvation of your soul, if you walk uprightly and do not regard iniquity in your heart, if you continue to wait patiently, and believingly upon God; then answers will surely be given to your prayers. You may not be called upon to serve the Lord in the way the writer does, and therefore may never have answers to prayer respecting such things as are recorded here; but, in your various circumstances, your family, your business, your profession, your church position, your labour for the Lord, etc., you may have answers as distinct as any here recorded."

THE GREAT NEED OF BEING SAVED BY FAITH IN CHRIST JESUS

"Should this, however, be read by any who are not believers in the Lord Jesus, but who are going on in the carelessness or self-righteousness of their unrenewed hearts, then I would affectionately and solemnly beseech such, first of all to be reconciled to God by faith in the Lord Jesus. You are sinners. You deserve punishment. If you do not see this, ask God to show it unto you. Let this now be your first and especial prayer. Ask God also to enlighten you not merely concerning your state by nature, but especially to reveal the Lord Jesus to your heart. God sent Him, that He might bear the punishment, due to us guilty sinners. God accepts the obedience and sufferings of the Lord Jesus, in the room of those who depend upon Him for the salvation of their souls; and the moment a sinner believes in the Lord Jesus, he obtains the forgiveness of all his sins. When thus he is reconciled to God, by faith in the Lord Jesus, and has obtained the forgiveness of his sins, he has boldness to enter into the presence of God, to make known his requests unto Him; and the more he is enabled to realize that his sins are forgiven, and that God, for Christ's sake, is well pleased with those who believe on Him, the more ready he will be to come with all his wants, both temporal and spiritual, to his Heavenly Father, that He may supply them. But as long as the consciousness of unpardoned guilt remains, so long shall we be kept at a distance from God, especially as it regards prayer. Therefore, dear reader, if you are an unforgiven sinner, let your first and especial prayer be, that God would be pleased to reveal to your heart the Lord Jesus, His beloved Son."

A DOUBLE ANSWER

"July 25 [1865]. — From the neighbourhood of London £100, with the following letter: 'My dear Sir, I believe that it is through the Lord's actings upon me, that I enclose you a cheque on the Bank of England, Western Branch, for £100. I hope that your affairs are going on well. Yours in the Lord * * * *.' This Christian gentleman, whom I have never seen, and who is engaged in a very large business in London, had sent me several times before a similar sum. A day or two before I received this last kind donation, I had asked the Lord, that He would be pleased to influence the heart of this donor to help me again, which I had never done before regarding him; and thus I had the double answer to prayer, in that not only money came in, but money from *him*. The reader will now see the meaning in the donor's letter, when he wrote 'I believe that it is through the Lord's actings upon me that I enclose you a cheque, &c.' Verily it was the Lord who acted upon this gentleman, to send me this sum. Perhaps the reader may think, that in acknowledging the receipt of the donation, I wrote to the donor what I have here stated. I did not. My reason for not doing so was, lest he should have thought I was in especial need, and might have been thus influenced to send more. In truly knowing the Lord, in really relying upon Him and upon Him alone, there is no need of giving hints directly or indirectly, whereby individuals may be induced further to help. I might have written to the donor (as was indeed the case), I need a considerable sum day by day for the current expenses of the various objects of the Institution, and also might have with truth told him, at that time, that I yet needed about Twenty Thousand Pounds, to enable me to meet all the expenses connected with the contemplated enlargement of the Orphan work. But my practice is, never to allude to any of these things in my correspondence with donors. When the Report is published, every one can see, who has a desire to see, how matters stand; and thus I leave things in the hands of God, to speak for us to the hearts of His stewards. And this He does. Verily we do not wait upon God in vain!"

CHRISTIANS IN BUSINESS

"Jan. 1 [1869]. — From Scotland £50 for Missions, £25 for the circulation of the Holy Scriptures, and £25 for the circulation of Tracts. Received also from a considerable distance £10 for these objects, with £10 for the Orphans. About this latter donation I make a few remarks. At the early part of the year 1868, a Christian business man wrote to me for advice in his peculiar difficult business affairs. His letter showed that he had a desire to walk in the ways of the Lord, and to carry on his business to the glory of God; but his circumstances were of the most trying character. I therefore wrote to him to come to Bristol, that I might be able to advise him. Accordingly he undertook the long journey, and I had an interview with him, through which I saw his most trying position in business. Having fully conversed with him, I gave him the following counsel: 1. That he should day by day, expressly for the purpose, retire with his Christian wife, that they might unitedly spread their business difficulties before God in prayer, and do this, if possible, twice a day. 2. That he should look out for answers to his prayers, and expect that God would help him. 3. That he should avoid all business trickeries, such as exposing for sale two or three articles, marked below cost price, for the sake of attracting customers, because of its being unbecoming a disciple of the Lord Jesus to use such artifices; and that, if he did so, he could not reckon on the blessing of God. 4. I advised him further, to set apart, out of his profits, week by week, a certain proportion for the work of God, whether his income was much or little, and use this income faithfully for the Lord. 5. Lastly, I asked him, to let me know, month after month, how the Lord dealt with him. — The reader will feel interested to learn, that from that time the Lord was pleased to prosper the business of this dear Christian brother, so that his returns from the 1st of March, 1868, up to March 1, 1869, were £9,138 13s. 5d., while during the same period the previous year they had been only £6,609 18s. 3d., therefore £2,528 15s. 2d. more than the year before. When he sent me the donation above referred to, he also writes, that he had been enabled to put aside during the previous year £123 13s. 3d. for the work of God or the need of the poor. — I have so fully dwelt on this, because Christians in business may be benefited by it."

REVIVAL IN THE ORPHAN-HOUSES

"In giving the statistics of the previous year [1871-72], I referred already to the great spiritual blessing, which it pleased the Lord to grant to the Orphan Work at the end of that year and the beginning of this; but, as this is so deeply important a subject, I enter somewhat further and more fully into it here. It was stated before, that the spiritual condition of the Orphans generally gave to us great sorrow of heart, because there were so few, comparatively, among them, who were in earnest about their souls, and resting on the atoning death of the Lord Jesus for salvation. This our sorrow led us to lay it on the whole staff of assistants, matrons and teachers, to seek earnestly the Lord's blessing on the souls of the children. This was done in our united prayer meetings, and I have reason to believe, in secret also; and in answer to these our secret and united prayers, in the year 1872, there were, as the result of this, more believers by far among the Orphans than ever. On Jan. 8, 1872, the Lord began to work among them, and this work was going on more or less afterwards. In the New Orphan-House No. 3, it showed itself least, till it pleased the Lord to lay His hand heavily on that house, by the small-pox; and, from that time the working of the Holy Spirit was felt in that house also, particularly in one department. At the end of July, 1872, I received the statements of all the matrons and teachers in the five houses, who reported to me, that, after careful observation and conversation, they had good reason to believe that 729 of the Orphans then under our care, were believers in the Lord Jesus. This number of believing Orphans is by far greater than ever we had, for which we adore and praise the Lord! See how the Lord overruled the great trial, occasioned by the small-pox, and turned it into a great blessing! See, also, how, after so low a state, comparatively, which led us to prayer, earnest prayer, the working of the Holy Spirit was more manifest than ever!"

MR. MÜELLER'S MISSION TOURS

In the year 1875, when seventy years of age, Mr. Müeller was led to start on his Missionary Tours, and during the next twenty years preached to more than three million people, in forty-two countries of the world.

"On August 8th, 1882," Mr. Müeller says, "we began our ninth Missionary Tour. The first place at which I preached was Weymouth, where I spoke in public four times. From Weymouth we went, by way of Calais and Brussels, to Dusseldorf on the Rhine, where I preached many times six years before. During this visit, I spoke there in public eight times. Regarding my stay at Dusseldorf, for the encouragement of the reader, I relate the following circumstance. During our first visit to that city, in the year 1876, a godly City Missionary came to me one day, greatly tried, because he had six sons, for whose conversion he had been praying many years, and yet they remained unconcerned about their souls, and he desired me to tell him what to do. My reply was, '*Continue* to pray for your sons, and *expect* an answer to your prayer, and you will have to praise God.' Now, when after six years I was again in the same city, this dear man came to me and said he was surprised he had not seen before himself what he ought to do, and that he had resolved to take my advice and more earnestly than ever give himself to prayer. Two months after he saw me, five of his six sons were converted within eight days, and have for six years now walked in the ways of the Lord, and he had hoped that the sixth son also was beginning to be concerned about his state before God. May the Christian reader be encouraged by this, should his prayers not at once be answered; and, instead of ceasing to pray, wait upon God all the more earnestly and perseveringly, and *expect* answers to his petitions."

THE DIVINE PLAN FOR SENDING OUT FOREIGN MISSIONARIES

The Bristol Church with which Mr. Müeller was connected has been privileged to set an example to the Church of God of the way in which Foreign Missionaries (who are so greatly needed) can be sent forth in answer to prayer. Mr. Müeller writes on p. 516, Vol. I. of his Narrative: —

"I also mention here, that during the eight years previous to my going to Germany to labour there, it had been laid on my heart, and on the hearts of some other brethren among us, to ask the Lord that we would be pleased to honour us, as a body of believers, by calling forth from our midst brethren, for carrying the truth into foreign lands. But this prayer seemed to remain unanswered. Now, however, the time has come when the Lord was about to answer it, and I, on whose heart particularly this matter had been laid, was to be the first to carry forth the truth from among us. About that very time the Lord called our dear brother and sister Barrington from among us, to go to Demerara, to labour there in connexion with our esteemed brother Strong, and our dear brother and sister Espenett, to go to Switzerland. Both these dear brethren and sisters left very shortly after I had gone to Germany. But this was not all. Our much valued brother Mordal, who had commended himself to the saints by his unwearied faithful service among us for twelve years, had from Aug. 31, 1843, (the day on which brothers Strong and Barrington sailed from Bristol for Demerara), his mind likewise exercised about service there, and went out from among us eleven months after. He, together with myself, had had it particularly laid upon his heart, during the eight years previously, to ask the Lord again and again to call labourers from among us for foreign service. Of all persons he, the father of a large family, and about 50 years of age, seemed the least likely to be called to that work; but God did call him. He went, laboured a little while in Demerara, and then, on January 9, 1845, the Lord took him to his rest. — When we ask God for a thing, such as that He would be pleased to raise up labourers for His harvest, or send means for the carrying on of His work, the honest question to be put to our hearts should be this: Am *I* willing to go, if He should call *me*? Am *I* willing to give according to *my* ability? For we may be the very persons whom the Lord will call for the work, or whose means He may wish to employ."

In the Report of the Scriptural Knowledge Institution for 1896 Mr. Müeller shows how greatly this body of believers has been honored by God.

"From our own midst as a church sixty brethren and sisters have gone forth to foreign fields of labour, some of whom have finished their labour on earth; but there are still about forty yet engaged in this precious service."

Why should not the great and crying need for workers in Asia, Africa, and other parts of the world be thus met by thousands of churches in Europe and America following this divine plan of praying the Lord of the harvest that He would send forth labourers from among them?

Surely they may expect GOD to answer their prayers as He did the prayers of this Bristol church.

Look what has been done in China by the faithful use of GOD's method! We quote Mr. Hudson Taylor's words as given in *China's Millions* for July, 1897: —

"For the obtaining of fellow-workers we took the MASTER's direction, 'Pray ye the Lord of the Harvest.' As for the first five before the Mission was formed, so for the twenty-four for whom we first asked for the C.I.M.; for further reinforcements when they were needed; for the seventy in three years, for the hundred in one year, and for further additions from time to time, we have ever relied on this plan. Is it possible that in any other way such a band of workers from nearly every denomination, and from many lands, could have been gathered and kept together for thirty years with no other bond save that which the call of GOD and the love of GOD has proved — a band now numbering over seven hundred men and women, aided by more than five hundred native workers."

THE BEGINNING OF THE 1859 REVIVAL

"In November, 1856, a young Irishman, Mr. James McQuilkin, was brought to the knowledge of the Lord. Soon after his conversion he saw my Narrative advertised, viz.: the first two volumes of this book. He had a great desire to read it, and procured it accordingly, about January, 1857. God blessed it greatly to his soul, especially in showing to him, what could be obtained by prayer. He said to himself something like this: 'See what Mr. Müeller obtains simply by prayer. Thus I may obtain blessing by prayer.' He now set himself to pray, that the Lord would give him a spiritual companion, one who knew the Lord. Soon after he became acquainted with a young man who was a believer. These two began a prayer-meeting in one of the Sunday Schools in the parish of Connor. Having his prayer answered in obtaining a spiritual companion, Mr. James McQuilkin asked the Lord to lead him to become acquainted with some more of His hidden ones. Soon after the Lord gave him two more young men, who were believers previously, as far as he could judge. In Autumn, 1857, Mr. James McQuilkin stated to these three young men, given him in answer to believing prayer, what blessing he had derived from my Narrative, how it had led him to see the power of believing prayer; and he proposed that they should meet for prayer to seek the Lord's blessing upon their various labours in the Sunday Schools, prayer-meetings, and preaching of the Gospel. Accordingly in Autumn, 1857, these four young men met together for prayer in a small school-house near the village of Kells, in the parish of Connor, every Friday evening. By this time the great and mighty working of the Spirit, in 1857, in the United States, had become known, and Mr. James McQuilkin said to himself, 'Why may not we have such a blessed work here, seeing that God did such great things for Mr. Müeller, simply in answer to prayer.' On January 1, 1858, the Lord gave them the first remarkable answer to prayer in the conversion of a farm servant. He was taken into the number, and thus there were five who gave themselves to prayer. Shortly after, another young man, about 20 years old, was converted; there were now six. This greatly encouraged the other three who first had met with Mr. James McQuilkin. Others now were converted, who were also taken into the number; but only believers were admitted to these fellowship meetings, in which they read, prayed, and offered to each other a few thoughts from the Scriptures. These meetings and others for the preaching of the Gospel were held in the parish of Connor, Antrim, Ireland. Up to this time all was going on most quietly, though many souls were converted. There were no physical prostrations, as afterwards.

"About Christmas, 1858, a young man, from Ahoghill, who had come to live at Connor, and who had been converted through this little company of believers, went to see his friends at Ahoghill, and spoke to them about their own souls, and the work of God at Connor. His friends desired to see some of these converts. Accordingly Mr. James McQuilkin, with two of the first who met for prayer, went on February 2, 1859, and held a meeting at Ahoghill in one of the Presbyterian Churches. Some believed, some mocked, and others thought there was a great deal of presumption in these young converts; yet many wished to have another meeting. This was held by the same three young men on February 16th, 1859; and now the Spirit of God began to work, and to work mightily. Souls were converted, and from that time conversions multiplied rapidly. Some of these converts went to other places, and carried the spiritual fire, so to speak, with them. The blessed work of the spirit of God spread in *many places*. — On April 5th, 1859, Mr. James McQuilkin went to Ballymena, held a meeting there in one of the Presbyterian Churches; and on April 11th held another meeting in another of the Presbyterian Churches. Several were convinced of sin and the work of the Spirit of God went forward in Ballymena. — On May 28th, 1859, he went to Belfast. During the first week there were meetings held in five different Presbyterian Churches, and from that time the blessed work commenced at Belfast. In all these visits he was accompanied and helped by Mr. Jeremiah Meneely, one of the three young men who first met with him, after the reading of my Narrative. From this time the work of the Holy Ghost spread further and further; for the young converts were used by the Lord to carry the truth from one place to another.

"Such was the *beginning* of that mighty work of the Holy Spirit, which has led to the conversion of hundreds of thousands; for some of my readers will remember how in 1859 this fire was kindled in England, Wales and Scotland; how it spread through Ireland, England, Wales and Scotland; how the Continent of Europe was more or less partaking of this mighty working of the Holy Spirit; how it led thousands to give themselves to the work of Evangelists; and how up to the year 1874 not only the effects of this work, first begun in Ireland, are felt, but that still more or less this blessed work is going on in Europe generally. It is almost needless to add, that in no degree the honour is due to the instruments, but to the Holy Spirit alone; yet these facts are stated, in order that it may be seen, what delight God has in answering abundantly the believing prayer of His children."

MR. MÜELLER'S MARRIAGE

In Vol. 3 of The Narrative, Mr. Müeller shows the ordering of God in his meeting with and subsequent marriage to his first wife, Miss Mary Groves.

"In giving her to me, I own the hand of God; nay, His hand was most marked; and my soul says, 'Thou art good, and doest good.'

"I refer to a few particulars for the instruction of others. When at the end of the year 1829, I left London to labour in Devonshire in the Gospel, a brother in the Lord gave to me a card, containing the address of a well-known Christian lady, Miss Paget, who then resided in Exeter, in order that I should call on her, as she was an excellent Christian. I took this address and put it into my pocket, but thought little of calling on her. Three weeks I carried this card in my pocket, without making an effort to see this lady; but at last I was led to do so. This was God's way of giving me my excellent wife. Miss Paget asked me to preach the last Tuesday in the month of January, 1830, at the room which she had fitted up at Poltimore, a village near Exeter, and where Mr. A. N. Groves, afterwards my brother-in-law, had preached once a month, before he went out as a Missionary to Bagdad. I accepted readily the invitation, as I longed, everywhere to set forth the precious truth of the Lord's return, and other deeply important truths, which not long before my own soul had been filled with.

"On leaving Miss Paget, she gave me the address of a Christian brother, Mr. Hake, who had an Infant Boarding School for young ladies and gentlemen, at Northernhay House, the former residence of Mr. A. N. Groves, in order that I might stay there on my arrival in Exeter from Teignmouth. To this place I went at the appointed time. Miss Groves, afterwards my beloved wife, was there; for Mrs. Hake had been a great invalid for a long time, and Miss Groves helped Mr. Hake in his great affliction, by superintending his household matters. My first visit led to my going again to preach at Poltimore, after the lapse of a month, and I stayed again at Mr. Hake's house; and this second visit led to my preaching once a week in a chapel at Exeter; and thus I went, week after week, from Teignmouth to Exeter, each time staying in the house of Mr. Hake. All this time my purpose had been, not to marry at all, but to remain free for travelling about in the service of the Gospel; but after some months I saw, for many reasons, that it was better for me, as a young Pastor, under 25 years of age, to be married. The question now was, to whom shall I be united? Miss Groves was before my mind; but the prayerful conflict was long, before I came to a decision; for I could not bear the thought, that I should take away from Mr. Hake this valued helper, as Mrs. Hake continued still unable to take the responsibility of so large a household. But I prayed again and again. At last this decided me, I had reason to believe that I had begotten an affection in the heart of Miss Groves for me, and that therefore I ought to make a proposal of marriage to her, however unkindly I might appear to act to my dear friend and brother Mr. Hake, and to ask God to give him a suitable helper to succeed Miss Groves. On Aug. 15th, 1830, I therefore wrote to her, proposing to her to become my wife, and on Aug. 19th, when I went over as usual to Exeter for preaching, she accepted me. The first thing we did, after I was accepted, was, to fall on our knees, and to ask the blessing of the Lord on our intended union. In about two or three weeks the Lord, in answer to prayer, found an individual, who seemed suitable to act as housekeeper, whilst Mrs. Hake continued ill; and on Oct. 7, 1830, we were united in marriage. Our marriage was of the most simple character. We walked to church, had no wedding breakfast, but in the afternoon had a meeting of Christian friends in Mr. Hake's house and commemorated the Lord's death; and then I drove off in the stagecoach with my beloved bride to Teignmouth, and the next day we went to work for the Lord. Simple as our beginning was, and unlike the habits of the world, for Christ's sake, so our Godly aim has been, to continue ever since. Now see the hand of God in giving me my dearest wife: — 1st, that address of Miss Paget's was given to me under the ordering of God. 2nd, I must at last be made to call on her, though I had long delayed it. 3rd, She might have provided a resting-place with some other Christian friend, where I should not have seen Miss Groves. 4th, My mind might have at last, after all, decided not to make a proposal to her; but God settled the matter thus in speaking to me through my conscience — you know that you have begotten affection in the heart of this Christian sister, by the way you have acted towards her, and therefore, painful though it may be, to appear to act unkindly towards your friend and brother, you ought to make her a proposal. I obeyed. I wrote the letter in which I made the proposal, and nothing but one even stream of blessing has been the result.

"Let me here add a word of Christian counsel. To enter upon the marriage union is one of the most deeply important events of life. It cannot be too prayerfully treated. Our happiness, our usefulness, our living for God or for ourselves afterwards, are often most intimately connected with our choice. Therefore, in the most prayerful manner, this choice should be made. Neither beauty, nor age, nor money, nor mental powers, should be that which prompt the decision; but 1st, Much waiting upon God for guidance should be used; 2nd, A hearty purpose, to be willing to be guided by Him should be aimed after; 3rd, True godliness without a shadow of doubt, should be the first and absolutely needful qualification to a Christian, with regard to a companion for life. In addition to this, however, it ought to be, at the same time, calmly and patiently weighed, whether, in other respects, there is a suitableness.

"For instance, for an educated man to choose an entirely uneducated woman, is unwise; for however much on his part love might be willing to cover the defect, it will work very unhappily with regard to the children."

DANGEROUS ILLNESS OF MR. MÜELLER'S DAUGHTER

"In July, 1853, it pleased the Lord to try my faith in a way in which before it had not been tried. My beloved daughter and only child, and a believer since the commencement of the year 1846, was taken ill on June 20th.

"This illness, at first a low fever, turned to typhus. On July 3rd there seemed no hope of her recovery. Now was the trial of faith. But faith triumphed. My beloved wife and I were enabled to give her up into the hands of the Lord. He sustained us both exceedingly. But I will only speak about myself. Though my only and beloved child was brought near the grave, yet was my soul in perfect peace, satisfied with the will of my Heavenly Father, being assured that He would only do that for her and her parents, which in the end would be the best. She continued very ill till about June 20th, when restoration began.

"On Aug. 18th she was so far restored that she could be removed to Clevedon for change of air, though exceedingly weak. It was then 59 days since she was first taken ill. * * * * * *

"Parents know what an only child, a beloved child is, and what to believing parents an only child, a believing child must be. Well, the Father in Heaven said, as it were, by this His dispensation, 'Art thou willing to give up this child to me?' My heart responded, As it seems good to Thee, my Heavenly Father. Thy will be done. But as our hearts were made willing to give back our beloved child to Him who had given her to us, so He was ready to leave her to us, and she lived. 'Delight thyself also in the Lord; and He shall give thee the desires of thine heart.' Psalm 37:4. The desires of my heart were, to retain the beloved daughter if it were the will of God; the means to retain her were to be satisfied with the will of the Lord.

"Of all the trials of faith that as yet I have had to pass through, this was the greatest; and by God's abundant mercy, I own it to His praise, I was enabled to delight myself in the will of God; for I felt perfectly sure, that, if the Lord took this beloved daughter, it would be best for her parents, best for herself, and more for the glory of God than if she lived: this better part I was satisfied with; and thus my heart had peace, perfect peace, and I had not a moment's anxiety. Thus would it be under all circumstances, however painful, were the believer exercising faith."

THE DAILY BREAD

"Aug. 3, 1844. Saturday. With the 12s. we began the day. My soul said: 'I will now look out for the way in which the Lord will deliver us this day again; for He will surely deliver. Many Saturdays, when we were in need, He helped us, and so He will do this day also.' Between nine and ten o'clock this morning I gave myself to prayer for means, with three of my fellow-labourers, in my house. WHILST WE WERE IN PRAYER, there was a knock at my room-door, and I was informed that a gentleman had come to see me. When we had finished prayer, it was found to be a brother from Tetbury, who had brought from Barnstaple £1 2s. 6d. for the Orphans. Thus we have £1 14s. 6d., with which I must return the letter-bag to the Orphan-Houses, looking to the Lord for more.

"Aug. 6 — Without *one single penny* in my hands the day began. The post brought nothing, nor had I yet received anything, when ten minutes after ten this morning the letter-bag was brought from the Orphan-Houses, for the supplies of to-day. — Now see the Lord's deliverance! In the bag I found a note from one of the labourers in the Orphan-Houses, enclosing two sovereigns, which she sent for the Orphans, stating that it was part of a present which she had just received unexpectedly, for herself. — Thus we are supplied for to-day.

"Sept. 4. — Only one farthing was in my hands this morning. Pause a moment, dear reader! Only one farthing in hand when the day commenced. Think of this, and think of nearly 140 persons to be provided for. You, poor brethren, who have six or eight children and small wages, think of this; and you, my brethren, who do not belong to the working classes, but have, as it is called, very limited means, think of this! May you not do, what we do, under your *trials*? Does the Lord love you less than He loves us? Does He not love all His children with no less love than that, with which He loves His only begotten Son, according to John 17:20-23? Or are we better than you? Nay, are we not in ourselves poor miserable sinners as you are; and have any of the children of God any claim upon God, on account of their own worthiness? Is not that, which alone can make us worthy to receive anything from our Heavenly Father, the righteousness of the Lord Jesus, which is imputed to those who believe in Him? Therefore, dear reader, as we pray in our every need, of whatever character it may be, in connection with this work, to our Father in Heaven for help, and as He does help us, so is He willing to help all His children who put their trust in Him. — Well, let us hear then, how God helped when there was only one farthing left in my hands, on the morning of Sept. 4, 1844.

"A little after nine o'clock I received a sovereign from a sister in the Lord, who does not wish the name of the place, where she resides, mentioned. Between ten and eleven o'clock the bag was sent from the Orphan-Houses, in which in a note it was stated that £1 2s. was required for to-day. SCARCELY HAD I READ THIS, when a fly stopped before my house, and a gentleman, Mr. _____, from the neighbourhood of Manchester, was announced. I found that he was a believer, who had come on business to Bristol. He had heard about the Orphan-Houses, and expressed his surprise, that without any regular system of collections, and without personal application to anyone, simply by faith and prayer, I obtained £2,000 and more yearly for the work of the Lord in my hands. This brother, whom I had never seen before; and whose name I did not even know before he came, gave me £2, as an exemplification of what I had stated to him."

"THE POOR WITH YOU ALWAYS"

"Feb. 12, 1845. — After I had sent off this morning the money which was required for the housekeeping of to-day, I had again only 16s. 2½d. left, being only about one-fourth as much as is generally needed for one day, merely for housekeeping, so that there was now again a fresh call for trusting in the Lord. In the morning I met again, as usual, with my dear wife and her sister, for prayer, to ask the Lord for many blessings in connection with this work, and for means also.

"About one hour after, I received a letter from Devonshire, containing an order for £22, of which £10 was for the Orphans, £2 for a poor brother in Bristol, and £10 for myself. — Besides having thus a fresh proof of the willingness of our Heavenly Father to answer our requests on behalf of the Orphans, there is this, moreover, to be noticed. For many months past, the necessities of the poor saints among us have been particularly laid upon my heart. The word of our Lord: 'Ye have the poor with you always,' and 'whensoever ye will ye may do them good,' has again and again stirred me up to prayer on their behalf, and thus it was again in particular this morning. It was the coldest morning we have had the whole winter. In my morning walk for prayer and meditation I thought how well I was supplied with coals, nourishing food, and warm clothing, and how many of the dear children of God might be in need; and I lifted up my heart to God to give me more means for myself, that I might be able, by actions, to show more abundant sympathy with the poor believers in their need; and it was but three hours after when I received this £10 for myself."

THE LORD DIRECTING THE STEPS

"Feb. 1, 1847. — Before breakfast I took a direction in my usual morning's walk, in which I had not been for many weeks, feeling drawn in that direction, just as if God had an intention in leading me in that way. Returning home I met a Christian gentleman whom formerly I used to meet almost every morning, but whom I had not met for many weeks, because I had not been walking in that direction. He stopped me and gave me £2 for the Orphans. Then I knew why I had been led thus; for there is not yet enough in hand, to supply the matrons to-morrow evening with the necessary means for housekeeping during another week.

"Feb. 4. — Yesterday nothing had come in. This morning, just before I was going to give myself to prayer about the Orphans, a sister in the Lord sent a sovereign, which she had received, as she writes, 'From a friend who had met the Orphan Boys, and was particularly pleased with their neat and orderly appearance.' After having received this £1, I prayed for means for present use, though not confining my prayers to that. About a quarter of an hour after I had risen from my knees, I received a letter, with an order for £5. The donor writes, that it is 'the proceeds of a strip of land, sold to the railway company.' What various means does the Lord employ to send us help, in answer to our prayers!"

CONTINUED TRIALS OF FAITH AND PATIENCE

With the enlargement of the work, by which some 330 persons needed to be provided for, the trials of faith continued. Mr. Müeller writes: —

"If we formerly had no certain income, so now have we none. We have to look to God for everything in connection with the work, of which often, however, the pecuniary necessities are the smallest matter; but to Him we are enabled to look and *therefore* it is, that we are not disappointed."

"Oct. 7, 1852. — This evening there was only £8 left in hand for the current expenses for the Orphans. Hitherto we had generally abounded. But though much had come in, since the commencement of this new period, yet our expenses had been greater than our income, as every donation almost of which the disposal was left with me, had been put to the Building Fund. Thus the balance in hand on May 26, 1852, notwithstanding the large income since then, was reduced to about £8. I therefore gave myself particularly to prayer for means, that this small sum might be increased.

"Oct. 9. — This morning Luke 7 came in the course of my reading before breakfast. While reading the account about the Centurion and the raising from death the widow's son at Nain, I lifted up my heart to the Lord Jesus thus: 'Lord Jesus, Thou hast the same power now. Thou canst provide me with means for Thy work in my hands. Be pleased to do so.' About half an hour afterwards I received £230 15s.

"The joy which such answers to prayer afford, cannot be described. I was determined to wait upon God only, and not to work an unscriptural deliverance for myself. I have thousands of pounds for the Building Fund; but I would not take of this sum because it was once set apart for that object. There is also a legacy of £100 for the Orphans two months overdue, in the prospect of the payment of which the heart might be naturally inclined to use some money of the Building Fund, to be replaced by the legacy money, when it comes in; but I would not thus step out of God's way of obtaining help. At the very time when this donation arrived, I had packed up £100 which I happened to have in hand; received for the Building Fund, in order to take it to the Bank, as I was determined not to touch it, but to wait upon God. My soul does magnify the Lord for His goodness.

"June 13, 1853. — We were now very poor. Not indeed in debt, nor was even all the money gone; for there was still about £12 in hand; but then there was needed to be bought flour, of which we buy generally 10 sacks at a time, 300 stones of oatmeal, 4 ctw. of soap, and there were many little repairs going on in the house, with a number of workmen, besides the regular current expenses of about £70 per week. Over and above all this, on Saturday, the day before yesterday, I found that the heading apparatus needed to be repaired, which would cost in all probability £25. It was therefore desirable, humanly speaking, to have £100 for these heavy extra expenses, besides means for the current expenses.

"But I had no human prospect whatever of getting even 100 pence, much less £100. In addition to this, to-day was Monday, when generally the income is little. But, in walking to the Orphan-House this morning, and praying as I went, I particularly told the Lord in prayer, that on this day, though Monday, He could send me much. And thus it was. I received this morning £301 for the Lord's service, as might be most needed. — The joy which I had cannot be described. I walked up and down in my room for a long time, tears of joy and gratitude to the Lord raining plentifully over my cheeks, praising and magnifying the

Lord for His goodness, and surrendering myself afresh, with all my heart, to Him for His blessed service. I scarcely ever felt more the kindness of the Lord in helping me.

"Nov. 9. — Our need of means is now great, very great. The Lord tries our faith and patience. This afternoon, a brother and sister in the Lord, from Gloucestershire, called to see me at the New Orphan-House, before going through the house. After a few minutes I received from the sister a sovereign, which she had been requested to bring to me for the Building Fund; and she gave me from herself £1 for my own personal expenses, and £1 for the Building Fund, and her husband gave me £5 for the Orphans, and £5 for Foreign Missions.

"Thus the Lord has refreshed my spirit greatly; but I look for more, and need much more.

"Nov. 12. — This evening, while praying for means, came a little parcel, containing ten sovereigns, from a Christian lady, living not far from the New Orphan-House. This was a very great refreshment to my spirit.

"Oct. 17, 1854. — This morning at family prayer, came, in the course of reading, Exodus 5, which shows that, just before the deliverance of the Israelites out of Egypt, their trials were greater than ever. They had not only to make the same number of bricks as before, but also to gather stubble, as no straw was given them any longer. This led me, in expounding the portion, to observe that even now the children of God are often in greater trial than ever, just before help and deliverance comes. Immediately after family prayer it was found, that by the morning's post not one penny had come in for the work of the Lord in which I am engaged, though we needed much, and though but very little had come in during the three previous days. Thus I had now to remember Exodus 5, and to practice the truths contained therein. In the course of the day nothing was received. In the evening I had, as usual, a season for prayer with my dear wife, respecting the various objects of the Scriptural Knowledge Institution, and then we left the New Orphan-House for our home.

"When we arrived at our house, about nine o'clock, we found that £5 and also 5s. had been sent from Norwich in two Post Office Orders for the Building Fund, and that £8 3s. 11d. had been sent in for Bibles, Tracts, and Reports, which had been sold. This called for thanksgiving. But a little later, between nine and ten o'clock, a Christian gentleman called and gave me £1 for the Orphans and £200 for foreign missions. He had received these sums from an aged Christian woman, whose savings as a servant, during her WHOLE life, made up the £200, and who, having recently had left to her a little annual income of about £30, felt herself constrained, by the love of Christ, to send the savings of her whole life for foreign missions.* * *

"Our especial prayer had been again and again, that the Lord would be pleased to send in means for missionary brethren, as I had reason to believe they were in much need of help; and only at eight o'clock this evening I had particularly besought the Lord to send help for this object. By the last mail I had sent off £40 to British Guiana, to help seven brethren there in some measure. This amount took the last pound in hand for this object. How gladly would I have sent assistance to other brethren also, but I had no more. Now I am in some degree supplied for this object.

"July 12, 1854. — Our means were now again reduced to about £30, as only about £150 had come in since June 15. In addition to this, we had very heavy expenses before us. This morning, in reading through the book of Proverbs, when I came to chapter 22:19 — 'That thy trust may be in the Lord, &C.,' I said in prayer to Him: 'Lord, I do trust in Thee; but wilt Thou now be pleased to help me; for I am in need of means for the current expenses of all the various objects of the Institution.' By the first delivery of letters I received an order on a London bank for £100, to be used for all the various objects 'as the present need might require.' "

ARE YOU PREPARED FOR ETERNITY?

"In looking over my account books, I meet again and again with the name of one and another who has finished his course. Soon, dear reader, your turn and mine may come. Are you prepared for eternity? Affectionately I press this question upon you. Do not put it away. Nothing is of greater moment than this point; yea, all other things, however important in their place, are of exceedingly small importance, in comparison with this matter. Do you ask, how you may be prepared for eternity, how to be saved, how to obtain the forgiveness of your sins? The answer is, believe in the Lord Jesus, trust in Him, depend upon Him alone as it regards the salvation of of your soul. He was punished by God, in order that we guilty sinners, if we believe in Him, might not be punished. He fulfilled the law of God, and was obedient even unto death, in order that we disobedient, guilty sinners, if we believe in Him, might, on His account, be reckoned righteous by God. Ponder these things, dear reader, should you have never done so before. Through faith in the Lord Jesus alone can we obtain forgiveness of our sins, and be at peace with God; but, believing in Jesus, we become, through this very faith, the children of God; have God as our Father, and may come to Him for all the temporal and spiritual blessings which we need. Thus everyone of my readers may obtain answers to prayers, not only to the same extent that we obtain them, but far more abundantly.

"It may be that few, comparatively, of the children of God are called to serve the Lord in the way of establishing Orphan-Houses, &C.; but all of them may, yea, are called upon to trust in God, to rely upon Him, in their various positions and circumstances, and apply the word of God, faith, and prayer to their family circumstances, their earthly occupation, their afflictions and necessities of every kind, both temporally and spiritually; just as we, by God's help, in some little measure seek to apply the word of God, faith, and prayer to the various objects of the Spiritual Knowledge Institution for Home and Abroad. Make but trial of it, if you have never done so before, and you will see how happy a life it is. * * * *

"Truly I prefer by far this life of almost constant trial, if I am only able to roll all my cares upon my Heavenly Father, and thus become increasingly acquainted with Him, to a life of outward peace and quietness, without these constant proofs of His faithfulness, His wisdom, His love, His power, His over-ruling providence, &C."

WAITING ONLY UPON GOD

"Sept. 6, 1854. — Received from Clerkenwell £50 to be used one-half for missions, and the other half as I thought best. I took the one-half for the support of the Orphans, and find the following remark in my journal respecting this donation: 'What a precious answer to prayer!' Since Aug. 26th we have been day by day coming to the Lord for our daily supplies. Precious, also, on account of Missionary brethren, whom I seek to help, for whom there was nothing in hand when this donation was received."

Mr. Müeller adds a few remarks to this part of the Narrative: —

"1. Should anyone suppose, on account of its having been stated in the previous pages that we were repeatedly brought low as to means, that the Orphans have not had all that was needful for them; we reply that *never*, since the work has been in existence, has there a mealtime come, but the Orphans have had good nourishing food in sufficient quantity: and never have they needed clothes, but I have had the means to provide them with all they required.

"2. Never since the Orphan work has been in existence have I asked one single human being for any help for this work; and yet, unasked for, simply in answer to prayer, from so many parts of the world, as has been stated, the donations have come in, and that very frequently at a time of the greatest need."

Mr. Müeller writes under date, 1859: —

"Every Wednesday evening I meet with my helpers for united prayer; and day by day I have stated seasons, when I seek to bring the work with its great variety of spiritual and temporal necessities, before the Lord in prayer, having perhaps each day 50 or more matters to bring before Him, and thus I obtain the blessing. I ask no human being for help concerning the work. Nay, if I could obtain £10,000 through each application for help; by God's grace, I would not ask. And why not? Because I have dedicated my whole life cheerfully to the precious service of giving to the world and to the church, a clear, distinct, and undeniable demonstration, that it is a blessed thing to trust in, and to wait upon, God; that He is now, as He ever was, the Living God, the same as revealed in the Holy Scriptures, and that if we know and are reconciled to Him through faith in the Lord Jesus, and ask Him in His name for that which is according to His mind, He will surely give it to us, in His own time, provided that we believe that He will. * * *

"Nor has God failed me at any time. Forty years have I proved His faithfulness, in this work."

IN THE LORD JEHOVAH IS EVERLASTING STRENGTH

Under date Nov. 9, 1861, Mr. Müeller wrote: —

"Nov. 9. Saturday evening. When this week commenced, I received only £3 19s. by the first delivery. Shortly after there came in the course of my reading, through the Holy Scriptures, Isaiah 26:4, 'Trust ye in the Lord for ever; for in the Lord Jehovah is everlasting strength.' — I laid aside my Bible, fell on my knees, and prayed thus: I believe that there is everlasting strength in the Lord Jehovah, and I do trust in Him; help me, O Lord, for ever to trust in Thee. Be pleased to give me more means this day, and much this week, though only so little now has come in. — That same day, Nov. 3rd, I received £10 from Surbiton, £5 from a donor residing in Clifton, £2 from a Bristol donor, and in the course of the week altogether £457 came in; thus Jehovah again proved, that in Him is everlasting strength, and that He is worthy to be trusted. — Dear believing reader, seek but in the same way to trust in the Lord, if you are not in the habit of doing so already, and you will find as I have found thousands of times, how blessed it is. But if the reader should be yet going on in carelessness about his soul, and therefore be without the knowledge of God and His dear Son, then the first, and most important thing, such a one has to do, is to trust in the Lord Jesus for the salvation of his soul, that he may be reconciled to God, and obtain the forgiveness of his sins."

JESUS CHRIST, THE SAME YESTERDAY, AND TO-DAY, AND FOREVER

"May 26, 1861. — At the close of the period I find, that the total expenditure for all the various objects was £24,700 16s. 4d., or £67 13s. 5¾d. per day, all the year round. During the coming year I expect the expenses to be considerably greater. But God, who has helped me these many years, will, I believe, help me in future also.

"You see, esteemed reader, how the Lord, in His faithful love helped us year after year. With every year the expenses increased, because the operations of the Institutions were further enlarged; but He never failed us. You may say, however, 'What would you do, if He should fail in helping you?' My reply is, that cannot be, as long as we trust in Him and do not live in sin. But if we were to forsake Him, the fountain of living waters, and to hew out to ourselves broken cisterns, which cannot hold water, by trusting in an arm of flesh; or if we were to live in sin, we should then have to call upon Him in vain, even though we professed still to trust in Him, according to that word: 'If I regard iniquity in my heart, the Lord will not hear me.' Psalm 66:18.

"Hitherto, by God's grace, I have been enabled to continue to trust in Him alone; and hitherto, though failing and weak in many ways, yet, by God's grace, I have been enabled to walk uprightly, hating sin and loving holiness, and longing after increased conformity to the Lord Jesus.

"Oct. 21, 1868. — As the days come, we make known our requests to Him, for our outgoings have now been for several years at the rate of more than One Hundred Pounds each day; but though the expenses have been so great, He has never failed us. We have been indeed, as to the outward appearance, like the 'Burning Bush in the Wilderness;' yet we have not been consumed. Moreover, we are full of trust in the Lord, and therefore of good courage, though we have before us the prospect, that, year by year, our expenses will increase more and more. Did all my beloved fellow disciples, who seek to work for God know the blessedness of looking truly to God alone, and trusting in Him alone, they would soon see how soul refreshing this way is, and how entirely beyond disappointment, so far as He is concerned. Earthly friends may alter their minds regarding the work in which we are engaged; but if indeed we work for God, whoever may alter His mind regarding our service, He will not. Earthly friends may lose their ability to help us, however much they may desire so to do; but He remains throughout eternity the infinitely Rich One. Earthly friends may have their minds after a time diverted to other objects, and, as they cannot help everywhere, much as they may desire it, they may, though reluctantly, have to discontinue to help us; but He is able, in all directions, though the requirements were multiplied a million times, to supply all that can possibly be needed, and does it with delight, where His work is carried on, and where He is confided in. Earthly friends may be removed by death, and thus we may lose their help, but He lives for ever, He cannot die. In this latter point of view, I have especially, during the past 40 years, in connection with this Institution, seen the blessedness of trusting in the Living God alone. Not one nor two, nor even five nor ten, but many more, who once helped me much with their means, have been removed by death; but have the operations of the Institution been stopped on that account? No. And how came this? Because I trusted in God, and in God alone."

THOROUGHLY IN HEART PREPARED FOR TRIALS OF FAITH

Under date July 28, 1874, Mr. Müeller wrote: —

"It has for months appeared to me, as if the Lord meant, by His dealings with us, to bring us back to that state of things, in which we were for more than ten years, from August, 1838, to April, 1849, when we had day by day, almost without interruption, to look to Him for our daily supplies, and, for a great part of the time, from meal to meal. The difficulties appeared to me indeed very great, as the Institution is now twenty times larger, than it was then, and our purchases are to be made in a wholesale way; but, at the same time, I am comforted by the knowledge, that God is aware of all this; and that, if this way be for the glory of His name, and for the good of His church and the unconverted world, I am, by His grace, willing to go this way, and to do it to the end of my course. The funds were thus fast expended; but God, our infinitely rich Treasurer, remains to us. It is this which gives me peace. Moreover, if it pleases Him, with a work requiring about £44,000 a year, to make me do again at the evening of my life, what I did from August, 1838, to April, 1849, I am not only prepared for it, but gladly again I would pass through all these trials of faith, with regard to means, if He only might be glorified, and His church and the world be benefited. Often and often this last point has of late passed through my mind, and I have placed myself in the position of having no means at all left, and Two Thousand and One Hundred persons not only daily at the table, but with everything else to be provided for, and all funds gone; 189 Missionaries to be assisted, and nothing whatever left; about one hundred schools, with about nine thousand scholars in them, to be entirely supported, and no means for them in hand; about Four Millions of Tracts and Tens of Thousands of copies of the Holy Scriptures yearly now to be sent out, and all the money expended. Invariably, however, with this probability before me, I have said to myself: 'God, who has raised up this work through me, God who has led me generally year after year to enlarge it, God who has supported this work now for more than forty years, will still help, and will not suffer me to be confounded, because I rely upon Him, I commit the whole work to Him, and He will provide me with what I need, in future also, though I know not, whence the means are to come.'

"Thus I wrote in my journal on July 28, 1874. The reader will now feel interested in learning how we fared under these circumstances.

"When I came home, last evening (July 27), I found letters had arrived, which contained £193, among which there was one from a

Missionary in Foreign lands, helped by the funds of this Institution, who, having come into the possession of some money, by the death of a relative, sent £153 0s. 4d. for Foreign Missions. This morning, July 28, came in £24 more, so that, when I met this afternoon with several of my helpers for prayer for means and various other matters, such as spiritual blessing upon the various Objects of the Institution, for more rain in this very dry season, the health of our fellow-labourers, etc., we had received, since yesterday afternoon, altogether £217. We thanked God for it, and asked for more. When the meeting for prayer was over, there was handed to me a letter from Scotland, containing £73 17s. 10d. and a paper with 13s. This was the immediate answer to prayer for more means.

"Aug. 12. — The income for this whole week, since Aug. 5, has been £897 15s. 6⅔d.

"Sept. 16. — Just after having again prayed for the payment of legacies, which have been left, I had a legacy receipt sent for the payment of a legacy for £1,800.

"Sept. 23. — Income to-day £5,365 13s. 6d., of which there was sent in one donation £5,327 7s. 6d. The Lord be praised!"

STRONG IN FAITH, GIVING GLORY TO GOD

On March 27, 1881, Mr. Müeller found that no money remained in hand for the School, Bible, Missionary and Tract Funds. Nearly £1,400 had been spent for these Objects during the previous month. He writes: —

"What was now to be done, dear reader, under these circumstances, when all the money for the above Objects was again gone? I reply, we did what we have done for 47 years, that is, we waited continually upon God. My dear fellow-labourers in Bristol, and my dear wife and myself in America, brought our necessities again and again before the Lord.

"Here in the United States, besides our habitual daily prayer for help, we had especial seasons 4, 5, and 6 times a day additionally, for pouring out our hearts before our Heavenly Father, and making known our requests unto Him, being assured that help would come: and we have not waited upon the Lord in vain. This plan may be despised by some, ridiculed by others, and considered insufficient by a third class of persons; but, under every trial and difficulty, we find prayer and faith to be our universal remedy; and, after having experienced for half a century their efficacy, we purpose, by God's help, to *continue* waiting upon Him, in order to show to an ungodly world, and to a doubting Church, that the Living God is still able and willing to answer prayer, and that it is the joy of His heart to listen to the supplications of His children. In Psalm 9:10, the Divine testimony regarding Jehovah is, 'They that know thy name will put their trust in Thee.' We know Him, by His grace, and do therefore put our trust in Him.

"April 27. — On March 27th we had no means at all in hand for these Objects, as stated under that date. We have now been helped through one more month, in answer to prayer, and have been supplied with all we need, though that amounted to nearly £1000, and have £23 8s. 6¼d. left.

"April 29. — A servant of the Lord Jesus, who, constrained by the love of Christ, seeks to lay up treasure in heaven, having received a legacy of £532 14s. 5d., gave £500 of it for these Objects.

"July 28, 1881. — The income has been for some time past only about the third part of the expenses. Consequently, all we have for the support of the Orphans is nearly gone; and for the first four Objects of the Institution we have nothing at all in hand. The natural appearance now is, that the work cannot be carried on. But I BELIEVE that the Lord will help, both with means for the Orphans and also for the other Objects of the Institution, and that we shall not be confounded; also, that the work shall not need to be given up. I am fully expecting help, and have written this to the glory of God, that it may be recorded hereafter for the encouragement of His children. The result will be seen.

"The foregoing was written at 7 A. M. July 28, 1881. As yet we have the means to meet our expenses, and I expect that we shall not be confounded, though for seven years we have not been so poor."

The result has indeed been seen, and will be seen. For more than 20 years since those words were written and Mr. Müeller had thus recorded his confidence in the Lord's help, God HAS sustained the work, and in May, 1902, there was a balance in hand of some thousands of pounds, notwithstanding that more than £500,000 had been received and expended since this entry was made in Mr. Müeller's journal on July 28, 1881.

During these 20 years faith and patience were at times greatly tried:

"Aug. 15, 1881. — The balance for the Orphans is now reduced to £332 12s. 7d., lower than it has been for more than twenty-five years. This sum we have in hand to meet the daily expenses in connection with 2,100 persons. It is only enough for the average outgoings of 4½ days. But our eyes are upon the Lord. I look to my heavenly Provider. The total income of to-day has been £28 5s. 2½ d.

"Aug. 22. — Part of a legacy, left years ago, £1,000, was paid, as the answer to many prayers.

"Feb. 26, 1882. — The balance in hand to-day for the Orphans is £97 10s. 7½d., viz. £24 more than the average expenses of one single day.

"March 2. — Our position now regarding the Orphan work is, praying day by day 'Give us *this day* our *daily* bread.' For a considerable time we have had day by day to look to the Lord for the supply of our *daily* wants; but God has helped us thus far.

"April 20, 1882. — When in the greatest need we received from Edinburgh £100 with this statement: 'The enclosed was intended as a legacy, but I have sent it in my lifetime.'

"June 3. — From Wottan-under-edge £500. A glorious deliverance was this donation, and a precious earnest of what God would do further for us.

"Oct. 21. — Received from Wottan-under-edge £1,000. * * * * * God, in answer to our prayers, spoke to His dear child, and inclined his heart to send to us more than ever. Thus He also gives proof, that during the previous year, when we were so low as to funds, it was only for the trial of our faith and patience, and not in anger; nor did He thereby mean to indicate, that He would not help us any more. For my own part, I *expected* further great help from God, and I have not been confounded.

"Aug. 17, 1883. — Our balance was reduced this afternoon to £10 2s. 7d. Think of this, dear reader! Day by day about 2,100 persons are to be provided for in the Orphan Institution, and £10 2s. 7d. was all that was in hand to do this. You see that we are just in the same position in which we were 46 years since as to funds. God is our banker. In Him we trust, and on Him we draw by faith. This was Saturday. In the evening £30 was received. On Monday we received £129 further, but had to pay out £60. On Tuesday we received £295, but had to pay out £180. * * * * *

"God is pleased continually to vary His mode of dealing with us, in order that we may not be tempted to trust in donors, or in circumstances, but in Him alone, and to keep our eye fixed upon Him. This, by His grace, we are enabled to do, and our hearts are kept in peace."

Some ten months later, when the balance in hand was only £41 10s., a very little more than one-half of the average expenses for the Orphans for one day, and there were sanitary operations advisable to be carried out, the expenses of which would amount to upwards of £2,000, Mr. Müeller received a legacy of £11,034 6s.

"June 7, 1884. — This is the largest donation I have *ever* received at *one time*. This legacy had been above six years in Chancery, and year after year its payment was expected, but remained unsettled by the Chancery Court. I kept on praying, however, and for six years prayed day by day that the money might be paid, believing that God in His own time *(which is always the best)*, would help at last; for *many* legacies in Chancery I had prayed out of the Court, and the money was eventually paid. In the present case, too, after faith and patience had been sufficiently exercised, God granted this request likewise."

1893. — In the Fifty-fourth Report of the Scriptural Knowledge Institution Mr. Müeller says: —

"The readers of the last report will remember under what particular trials we entered upon the last financial year of the Institution, from May 26th, 1892, to May 26th, 1893; but we trusted in *God*; with unshaken confidence we looked to *Him*, and we *expected* that we should somehow or other be helped. * * While thus we went on, my heart was at peace habitually, being assured that all this was permitted by God, to prepare a blessing for thousands, who would afterwards read the record of His dealings with us, during the year from May 26th, 1892, to May 26th, 1893. With reference to our dear fellow-labourers, Mr. Wright and I have seen already, while passing through the trial, how God has blessed it to them.

"Aug. 30, 1892. — This evening, whilst reading in the Psalms, I came to Psalm 81:10, and remembered the work of the Holy Spirit in my heart, when reading this verse on Dec. 5, 1835, and the effect which this had, not only on leading me to found the greatest Orphan Institution in the world, but I thought also of the blessing which has thus been brought to tens of thousands of believers and unbelievers all over the world. Putting aside the Bible, therefore, I fell on my knees and asked God that He would graciously be pleased to repeat His former kindness, and to supply me again more abundantly with means. Accordingly in less than half an hour, I received £50 from a Bristol Donor and from Redland a large quantity of fish, in addition to £97 already received to-day as the result of much prayer. By the last delivery, at 9 p. m., I received £5 more also, and had thus £152 in all, this day, as the result of prayer.

"Nov. 11. — There came in to-day, by the first two deliveries, only about £9, but the Lord increased the income to more than £200 this day. I am never discouraged by very little only coming in, but say to myself, and also to my dear helpers, 'More prayer, more patience, and more exercise of faith will bring greater blessing'; for thus I have invariably found it, since October, 1830, now 63 years ago, when I first began this life of entire dependence upon God for everything.

"March 1, 1893. — The income during this week, ending to-day, was £92 8s. 8¾d. for the Orphans, and £9 11s. 2d. for the other Objects, being about the sixth part of our weekly expenses; but now the great trial of our faith was nearly brought to a close, as will presently be seen.

"March 4. — *This very day* God begins to answer our prayers, as we have received a very good offer for the land we have to sell, even £1,000 per acre. The beginning of the day was darker as to outward appearances than ever: but we trusted in God for help. The first three deliveries of letters brought us only £4, and the remaining three brought us so little that the whole day's income was only £8 instead of £90, the amount we require every day to meet all our expenses. But God has now helped us. We have been able this evening to sell ten acres of land and two-fifths of an acre at £1,000 per acre, and shall receive £10,405 altogether for the whole of one field. The contract was signed at 8 o'clock this evening."

MR. MÜELLER'S DEPARTURE TO BE WITH CHRIST

On the evening of Wednesday, March 9th, 1898, Mr. Müeller took part in the usual meeting for prayer held in the Orphan-House No. 3; retired at his usual hour to rest, and early on the following morning (the 10th of March) alone, in his bed-room, breathed his last, realizing what had long been with him a most joyous anticipation, viz., that "to depart and to be with Christ is far better."

March 14. — This day Mr. Müeller's earthly remains were laid in the grave of his first and second wives, at Arno' Vale Cemetery. The attendant circumstances, throughout, were very remarkable and interesting to the Christian mind chiefly as illustrating God's eternal principle — "Them that honour Me I will honour." The man who in life sought not his own glory, became in death the one to whom all classes delighted to show respect and honour.

From the masses of sympathizing spectators that lined the streets, from the tearful eyes, and the audible prayerful ejaculations that escaped the lips of bystanders (many of them the poorest of the poor), as the orphans filed past, following the hearse; from the suspension of all traffic in the principal streets, the tolling of muffled bells, and the half-masted flags, and from the dense crowds in the cemetery that awaited the arrival of the funeral company, it seemed as if the whole city had spontaneously resolved to do honour to the man who had not lived for himself, but for the glory of God and the good of his fellows.

For some 21 months before Mr. Müeller's death the trials of faith and patience were great. Mr. James Wright, Mr. Müeller's successor, writes:

"He who is pleased, sometimes, to teach His servants 'how to *abound,*' sees it *best* for them, at other times 'to be instructed how to suffer need.' For many of the 64 years during which this work has been carried on, the former was our experience; we abounded and richly abounded, latterly, and especially during the last 2 or 3 years it has been the very reverse. *Pressing need* has been the *rule;* a balance in hand, over and above our need, the rare exception. Yet we have never been forsaken."

"Sept. 23, 1897. — Residue of the legacy of the late G. J., Esq., £2,679 18s. 7d. This sum was received when we were in the *deepest need;* and after it had pleased the Lord to allow a very protracted trial of faith and patience; but see, beloved reader, He did not disappoint nor forsake us, as He *never* does those who really trust in Him. The *joy* of *such* a deliverance cannot be tasted without the experience of the previous *trial.*

"Feb. 26, 1898. — The following entry, under this date, is in Mr. Müeller's own hand-writing:

PRECIOUS ANSWERS TO PRAYER

"The income to-day, by the two first deliveries, was £7 15s. 11d. Day by day our great trial of faith and patience continues, and thus it has been, more or less, now, for 21 months, yet, by Thy grace, we are sustained."

March 1, 1898. — The following, again, is from a memorandum in Mr. Müeller's own hand-writing, under this date:

"For about 21 months with scarcely the least intermission the trial of our faith and patience has continued. Now, to-day, the Lord has refreshed our hearts. This afternoon came in, for the Lord's work, £1,427 1s. 7d. as part payment of a legacy of the late Mrs. E. C. S. For 3 years and 10 months this money has been in the Irish Chancery Court. Hundreds of petitions had been brought before the Lord regarding it, and now at last, this portion of the total legacy has been received."

Thus the Lord, in love and faithfulness, greatly refreshed the heart of His servant, only nine days before taking him home to be with Himself.

Appendix A
FIVE CONDITIONS OF PREVAILING PRAYER

ENTIRE DEPENDENCE upon the merits and mediation of the Lord Jesus Christ, as the only ground of any claim for blessing. (See John 14:13, 14; 15:16, etc.)

2. — Separation from all known sin. If we regard iniquity in our hearts, the Lord will not hear us, for it would be sanctioning sin. (Psalm 66:18.)

3. — Faith in God's word of promise as confirmed by His oath. Not to believe Him is to make Him both a liar and a perjurer. (Hebrews 11:6; 6:13-20.)

4. — Asking in accordance with His will. Our motives must be godly: we must not seek any gift of God to consume it upon our lusts. (I John 5:14; James 4:3.)

5. — Importunity in supplication. There must be waiting on God and waiting for God, as the husbandman has long patience to wait for the harvest. (James 5:7; Luke 18:1-8.)

Appendix B
THE CAREFUL AND CONSECUTIVE READING OF THE HOLY SCRIPTURES

CONCERNING THIS SUBJECT Mr. Müeller says: "I fell into the snare, into which so many young believers fall, the reading of religious books in preference to the Scriptures. I could no longer read French and German novels, as I had formerly done, to feed my carnal mind; but still I did not put into the room of those books the best of all books. I read tracts, missionary papers, sermons, and biographies of godly persons. The last kind of books I found more profitable than others, and had they been well selected, or had I not read too much of such writings, or had any of them tended particularly to endear the Scriptures to me, they might have done me much good. — I never had been at any time in my life in the habit of reading the Holy Scriptures. When under fifteen years of age, I occasionally read a little of them at school; afterwards God's precious book was entirely laid aside, so that I never read one single chapter of it, as far as I remember, till it pleased God to begin a work of grace in my heart. Now the Scriptural way of reasoning would have been: God himself has condescended to become an author, and I am ignorant about that precious book, which His Holy Spirit has caused to be written through the instrumentality of His servants, and it contains that which I ought to know, and the knowledge of which will lead me to true happiness; therefore I ought to read again and again this most precious book, this book of books, most earnestly, most prayerfully, and with much meditation; and in this practice I ought to continue all the days of my life. For I was aware, though I read it but little, that I knew scarcely anything of it. But instead of acting thus, and being led by my ignorance of the word of God to study it more, my difficulty in understanding it, and the little enjoyment I had in it, made me careless of reading it (for much prayerful reading of the Word, gives not merely more knowledge, but increases the delight we have in reading it); and thus, like many believers, I practically preferred, for the first four years of my divine life, the works of uninspired men to the oracles of the living God. The consequence was, that I remained a babe, both in knowledge and grace. In knowledge I say; for all *true* knowledge must be derived, by the Spirit, from the Word. And as I neglected the Word, I was for nearly four years so ignorant, that I did not *clearly* know even the *fundamental* points of our holy faith. And this lack of knowledge most sadly kept me back from walking steadily in the ways of God. For it is the truth that makes us free, (John 8:31, 32,) by delivering us from the slavery of the lusts of the flesh, the lusts of the eyes, and the pride of life. The Word proves it. The experience of the saints proves it; and also my own experience most decidedly proves it. For when it pleased the Lord in Aug. 1829, to bring me really to the Scriptures, my life and walk became very different. And though even since that I have very much fallen short of what I might and ought to be, yet, by the grace of God, I have been enabled to live much nearer to Him than before.

"If any believers read this, who practically prefer other books to the Holy Scriptures, and who enjoy the writings of men much more than the word of God, may they be warned by my loss. I shall consider this book to have been the means of doing much good, should it please the Lord, through its instrumentality, to lead some of His people no longer to neglect the Holy Scriptures, but to give them that preference, which they have hitherto bestowed on the writings of men. My dislike to increase the number of books would have been sufficient to deter me from writing these pages, had I not been convinced, that this is the only way in which the brethren at large may be benefited through my mistakes and errors, and been influenced by the hope, that in answer to my prayers, the reading of my experience may be the means of leading them to value the Scriptures more highly, and to make them the rule of all their actions. * * *

"If anyone should ask me, how he may read the Scriptures most profitably, I would advise him, that:

"I. — Above all he should seek to have it settled in his own mind, that God alone, by His Spirit, can teach him, and that therefore, as God will be enquired of for blessings, it becomes him to seek God's blessing previous to reading, and also whilst reading.

"II. — He should have it, moreover, settled in his mind, that, although the Holy Spirit is the *best* and *sufficient* teacher, yet that this teacher does not always teach immediately when we desire it, and that, therefore, we may have to entreat Him again and again for the explanation of certain passages; but that He will surely teach us at last, if indeed we are seeking for light prayerfully, patiently, and with a view to the glory of God.

"III. — It is of immense importance for the understanding of the word of God, to read it in course, so that we may read every day a portion of the Old and a portion of the New Testament, going on where we previously left off. This is important — 1. Because it throws light upon the connection; and a different course, according to which one *habitually* selects particular chapters, will make it utterly impossible ever to understand much of the Scriptures. 2. Whilst we are in the body, we need a change even in spiritual things; and this change the Lord has graciously provided in the great variety which is to be found in His word. 3. It tends to the glory of God; for the leaving out some chapters here and there, is practically saying, that certain portions are better than others: or, that there are certain parts of revealed truth unprofitable or unnecessary. 4. It may keep us, by the blessing of God, from erroneous views, as in reading thus regularly through the Scriptures we are led to see the meaning of the whole, and also kept from laying too much stress upon certain favorite views. 5. The Scriptures contain the whole revealed will of God, and therefore we ought to seek to read from time to time through the whole of that revealed will. There are many believers, I fear, in our day, who have not read even once through the whole of the Scriptures; and yet in a few months, by reading only a few chapters every day they might accomplish it.

"IV. — It is also of the greatest importance to meditate on what we read, so that perhaps a small portion of that which we have read, or, if we have time, the whole may be meditated upon in the course of the day. Or a small portion of a book, or an epistle, or a gospel, through which we go regularly for meditation, may be considered every day, without, however, suffering oneself to be brought into bondage by this plan.

"Learned *commentaries* I have found to store the *head*, with many notions and often also with the truth of God; but when the *Spirit* teaches, through the instrumentality of prayer and meditation, the *heart* is affected. The former kind of knowledge generally puffs up, and is often renounced, when another commentary gives a different opinion, and often also is found good for nothing, when it is to be carried out into practice. The latter kind of knowledge generally humbles, gives joy, leads us nearer to God, and is not easily reasoned away; and having been obtained from God, and thus having entered into the heart, and become our own, is also generally carried out."

Appendix C
PROVING THE ACCEPTABLE WILL OF GOD

IT IS VERY INSTRUCTIVE and helpful to see the way in which Mr. Müeller proved the acceptable will of the Lord, when exercised in heart about the enlargement of the Orphan work, so that not only 300 but 1000 Orphans might be provided for.

"Dec. 11, 1850. — The especial burden of my prayer therefore is, that God would be pleased to teach me His will. My mind has also been especially pondering, how I could know His will satisfactorily concerning this particular. Sure I am, that I shall be taught. I therefore desire patiently to wait for the Lord's time, when He shall be pleased to shine on my path concerning this point.

"Dec. 26. — Fifteen days have elapsed since I wrote the preceding paragraph. Everyday since then I have continued to pray about this matter, and that with a goodly measure of earnestness, by the help of God. There has passed scarcely an hour during these days, in which, whilst awake, this matter has not been more or less before me. But all without even a shadow of excitement. I converse with no one about it. Hitherto have I not even done so with my dear wife. From this I refrain still, and deal with God alone about the matter, in order that no outward influence, and no outward excitement may keep me from attaining unto a clear discovery of His will. I have the fullest and most peaceful assurance, that He will clearly show me His will. This evening I have had again an especial solemn season for prayer, to seek to know the will of God. But whilst I continue to entreat and beseech the Lord, that He would not allow me to be deluded in this business, I may say I have scarcely any doubt remaining on my mind as to what will be the issue, even that I should go forward in this matter.

"As this, however, is one of the most momentous steps that I have ever taken, I judge that I cannot go about this matter with too much caution, prayerfulness, and deliberation. I am in no hurry about it. I could wait for years, by God's grace, were this His will, before even taking one single step towards this thing, or even speaking to anyone about it; and, on the other hand, I would set to work to-morrow, were the Lord to bid me do so. This calmness of mind, this having no will of my own in the matter, this only wishing to please my Heavenly Father in it, this only seeking His and not my honour in it; this state of heart, I say, is the fullest assurance to me that my heart is not under a fleshly excitement, and that, if I am helped thus to go on, I shall know the will of God to the full. But, while I write thus, I cannot but add at the same time, that I do crave the honour and the glorious privilege to be more and more used by the Lord. I have served Satan much in my younger years, and I desire now with all my might to serve God, during the remaining days of my earthly pilgrimage. I am forty-five years and three months old. Every day decreases the number of days that I have to stay on earth. I therefore desire with all my might to work. There are vast multitudes of Orphans to be provided for. * * *

"I desire that thus it may be more abundantly manifest that God is still the hearer and answerer of prayer, and that He is the living God now, as He ever was and ever will be, when He shall, simply in answer to prayer, have condescended to provide me with a house for 700 Orphans, and with means to support them. This last consideration is the most important point in my mind. The Lord's honour is the principal point with me in this whole matter; and just because that is the case, if He would be more glorified by my not going forward in this business, I should, by His grace, be perfectly content to give up all thoughts about another Orphan-House. Surely, in such a state of mind, obtained by the Holy Spirit, Thou, O my Heavenly Father, will not suffer Thy child to be mistaken, much less to be deluded! By the help of God I shall continue further, day by day, to wait upon Him in prayer concerning this thing, till He shall bid me act.

"Jan. 2, 1851. — A week ago I wrote the preceding paragraph. During this week I have still been helped, day by day, and more than once every day to seek the guidance of the Lord about another Orphan-House. The burden of my prayer has still been, that He, in His great mercy, would keep me from making a mistake. During the last week the Book of Proverbs has come in the course of my Scripture reading, and my heart has been refreshed, in reference to this subject, by the following passages: 'Trust in the Lord with all thine heart; and lean not unto thine own understanding. In all thy ways acknowledge Him, and

He shall direct thy paths.' Prov. 3:5, 6. By the grace of God I do acknowledge the Lord in my ways, and in this thing in particular; I have therefore the comfortable assurance that He will direct my paths concerning this part of my service, as to whether I shall be occupied in it or not. Further: 'The integrity of the upright shall preserve them; but the perverseness of fools shall destroy them.' Prov. 11:3. By the grace of God I am upright in this business. My honest purpose is to get glory to God. Therefore I expect to be guided aright. Further: 'Commit thy works unto the Lord and thy thoughts shall be established.' Prov. 16:3. I do commit my works unto the Lord, and therefore expect that my thoughts will be established. — My heart is more and more coming to a calm, quiet, and settled assurance, that the Lord will condescend to use me yet further in the Orphan Work. Here, Lord, is Thy servant!"

Mr. Müeller wrote down eight reasons against and eight reasons for establishing another Orphan-House for Seven Hundred Orphans.

The following is his last reason for so doing:

"I am peaceful and happy, spiritually, in the prospect of enlarging the work as on former occasions when I had to do so. This weighs particularly with me as a reason for going forward. After all the calm, quiet, prayerful consideration of the subject for about eight weeks, I am peaceful and happy, spiritually, in the purpose of enlarging the field. This, after all the heart searching which I have had, and the daily prayer to be kept from delusion and mistake in this thing, and the betaking myself to the Word of God, would not be the case, I judge, had not the Lord purposed to condescend to use me more than ever in this service.

"I, therefore, on the ground of the objections answered, and these eight reasons FOR enlarging the work, come to the conclusion that it is the will of the blessed God, that His poor and most unworthy servant should yet more extensively serve Him in this work, which he is quite willing to do."

"May 24. — From the time that I began to write down the exercises of my mind on Dec. 5th, 1850, till this day, ninety-two more Orphans have been applied for, and seventy-eight were already waiting for admission before. But this number increases rapidly as the work becomes more and more known.

"On the ground of what has been recorded above, I purpose to go forward in this service, and to seek to build, to the praise and honor of the living God another Orphan-House, large enough to accommodate seven hundred Orphans."

INSPIRATIONAL LIBRARY

Beautiful purse/pocket size editions of Christian Classics bound in flexible leatherette or genuine Bonded Leather. The Bonded Leather editions have gold edges and make beautiful gifts.

THE BIBLE PROMISE BOOK Over 1000 promises from God's Word arranged by topic. What does the Bible promise about matters like: Anger, Illness, Jealousy, Sex, Money, Old Age, et cetera, et cetera.
  Flexible Leatherette .... $ 3.95
  Genuine Bonded Leather $10.95

DAILY LIGHT One of the most popular daily devotionals with readings for both morning and evening. One page for each day of the year.
  Flexible Leatherette .... $ 4.95
  Genuine Bonded Leather $10.95

WISDOM FROM THE BIBLE Daily thoughts from the Proverbs which communicate truth about ourselves and the world around us. One page for each day in the year.
  Flexible Leatherette .... $ 4.95
  Genuine Bonded Leather $10.95

MY DAILY PRAYER JOURNAL Each page is dated and has a Scripture verse and ample room for you to record your thoughts, prayers and praises. One page for each day of the year.
  Flexible Leatherette .... $ 4.95
  Genuine Bonded Leather $10.95

Available wherever books are sold.

or order from:
Barbour and Company, Inc.
164 Mill Street   Box 1219
Westwood, New Jersey   07675

If you order by mail add $1.00 to your order for shipping.
Prices subject to change without notice.

HEROES OF THE FAITH

Biographies of great Christians in deluxe, hardcover, gold stamped, gift editions. These beautifully crafted columes are in matching blue leatherette bindings so you can purchase a complete set or pick and choose. All books are complete and unabridged and are printed in good readable print.

Only $7.95 each!

John Bunyan

Fanny Crosby

David Livingstone

Martin Luther

Dwight L. Moody

George Müller

Mary Slessor

John Wesley

Available wherever books are sold.

Or order from:
Barbour and Company, Inc.
164 Mill Street, Box 1219
Westwood, New Jersey 07675

If you order by mail add $2.00 to your order for shipping.
Prices subject to change without notice.